TOWER AIR FRY
COOKBOOK FOR BEGINNERS

Affordable Tower Air Fryer Recipes, a Variety of Delicious, Fried Dishes

TABLE OF CONTENTS

FISH & SEAFOOD RECIPES...43

DESSERTS RECIPES 54

VEGETABLE & & VEGETARIAN RECIPES 97

INTRODUCTION

An air fryer is a kitchen appliance that cooks food by using hot air instead of lots of oil. It is considered a healthier alternative to deep-frying. IT also acts as a small and more time-effective oven for baking. Instead of submerging food in oil, an air fryer uses a fan to circulate hot air around the food, creating that familiar crispy, golden-brown exterior. Air fryers come in various sizes and shapes, from small countertop models to larger ones that can cook a whole chicken.

WHY USE AN AIR FRYER?

Healthier Cooking: As mentioned earlier, air frying uses little to no oil, making it a healthier alternative to deep-frying. It is a great way to enjoy your favorite fried foods without the guilt.

Time-saving: Air fryers cook food faster than traditional methods, such as baking or frying. They also require less cleanup.

Versatile: Air fryers can cook a wide variety of foods, from vegetables to meats to desserts. They are also great for reheating leftovers, as they can revive the crispiness of fried foods.

WHY AN AIR FRYER SO POPULAR?

The popularity of air fryers can be attributed to several factors:

Health consciousness: As more people become health-conscious, air fryers provide a way to enjoy fried foods without the added calories and fat.

Convenience: Air fryers are easy to use, cook fast and require minimal cleanup.

Social media influence: The rise of social media influencers and their endorsement of air fryers has contributed to its popularity. Many influencers share recipes and cooking tips, showcasing the versatility of air fryers.

MOST POPULAR THINGS TO AIR FRY

Here are some of the most popular things we cook in the air fryer:

French fries: Crispy, golden-brown fries are a classic air fryer recipe.

Chicken wings: Air fryer chicken wings are crispy on the outside and juicy on the inside. Coat the wings with your favorite sauce, and air fry until crispy. Kiddos also love chicken nuggets.

Vegetables: Air fryers are great for roasting vegetables, such as Brussels sprouts, broccoli and cauliflower. Simply spray with a little olive oil and seasoning, and air fry until tender.

Fish: Air fryers can cook fish filets, such as salmon or tilapia, to perfection. Coat the fish with breadcrumbs or a seasoning blend, and air fry until crispy.

Desserts: Air fryers can even be used to make desserts, such as churros, doughnuts and more!

FAQS ABOUT AIR FRYERS

Is air frying healthier than deep frying?
Yes, air frying is generally considered healthier than deep frying, as it uses little to no oil.

Do I need to preheat the air fryer?
Yes, it is recommended to preheat the air fryer for a few minutes before cooking. This ensures that the air fryer is at the optimal temperature for cooking and helps to prevent uneven cooking. My air fryer has a preheat button right on it!

How much can an air fryer hold?
The answer to this really depends on the model you purchase. Some smaller air fryers can hold up to 2 quarts, while larger ones can hold up to 8 quarts. It is important to check the capacity of your air fryer before cooking to ensure that you do not overcrowd the basket. For your air fryer to cook properly, you will want a single layer of food.

Do I need to purchase extras and attachments for my air fryer?
It is not necessary to purchase extras or attachments for your air fryer, but they can be useful. Some popular accessories include baking pans, grilling racks, and skewers.

How do I prevent food from sticking to my air fryer?
To prevent food from sticking to your air fryer, lightly coat it with cooking spray or oil before cooking. You can also coat the food with a thin layer of oil or use a non-stick cooking spray.

HOW DO I CLEAN MY AIR FRYER?
To clean your air fryer, follow these steps:
1. Unplug it and let it cool completely.
2. Remove the basket and any of the other removable parts.
3. Wash the removable parts in warm soapy water. Pro Tip: Be sure you're using a sponge that is not abrasive. Otherwise you could scratch the non-stick coating.
4. Finally, wipe the inside of your appliance with a damp cloth or sponge. Do not use harsh chemicals or abrasive cleaners on your air fryer.
5. Let it dry completely before using it again.

TIPS FOR GETTING THE BEST RESULTS

1. Preheat the air fryer before adding your food. This will ensure that the temperature is consistent and your food cooks evenly.

2. Don't overcrowd the air fryer basket. Leave some space around each piece of food to allow for proper air circulation and to ensure that everything cooks evenly. You can always cook in batches if necessary.

3. Turn the food. The top portion of the food always crisps more than the underside, so it's super important to rotate everything in the basket part-way through cooking. To air fry small items shake the basket periodically over the cooking time to help ensure even cooking and browning. For larger pieces, like when air frying turkey burgers, flip them halfway through so that the top and bottom both crisp up.

4. It's not oil-free cooking. It's just not as much oil as deep frying. Use a light mist of cooking spray or brush a small amount of oil onto your food to help it crisp up and prevent sticking.

5. Experiment with cooking times and temperatures to find the sweet spot for your favorite foods. Keep notes on what works well for you so you can replicate your successes in the future.

6. Clean your air fryer every time to prevent smoky buildup of grease and food particles. Refer to the manufacturer's instructions for specific cleaning recommendations.

BREAKFAST & BRUNCH RECIPES

Sausage & Egg Breakfast Pockets

Ingredients:
- Dough:
- 1 cup Greek yogurt
- 1 cup self-rising flour
- Garlic powder, to tasteFor filling:
- 5 eggs, scrambled
- 1 egg + 1 Tbsp of water to make egg wash
- 6 oz cooked turkey sausage
- 1 cup fat-free shredded cheese

Directions:
1. Combine all dough ingredients into a medium-sized bowl. Knead together by hand or using the dough hook attachment of a stand mixer. If the dough is too sticky, add up to one tablespoon of flour.
2. Divide the dough into quarters. On a lightly floured surface, roll out into circles.
3. Add ¼ of the scrambled eggs and ¼ of the sausage each of the rolled-out circles. Top with ¼ cup of cheese.
4. Pinch the circles closed to form pockets. Brush each pocket with egg wash.
5. Air fry at 370° for 6 minutes. Flip and air fry for 6 additional minutes. Enjoy!

Baked Custard Toasts
Servings: 4

Ingredients:
- ½ cup Greek yogurt
- 1 large egg
- 1½ tablespoons maple syrup
- ½ teaspoon ground cinnamon
- ½ teaspoon vanilla extract
- ¼ teaspoon ground ginger
- ¼ teaspoon kosher salt
- 4 slices brioche, thick-cut
- 20 blackberries
- 2 tablespoons powdered sugar, for dusting
- 1 tablespoon fresh mint leaves, chopped, for garnish

Directions:
1. Whisk the Greek yogurt, egg, maple syrup, cinnamon, vanilla extract, ginger, and salt together in a small bowl to make the custard.
2. Use your fingers to gently press a well in the center of each piece of brioche. Fill each well with the yogurt custard, then place 5 blackberries into the custard of each slice.
3. Place the crisper plate into the Smart Air Fryer basket.
4. Select the Preheat function, adjust temperature to 325°F, then press Start/Pause.
5. Place 2 brioche slices onto the preheated crisper plate.
6. Set temperature to 325°F and time to 8 minutes, then press Start/Pause.
7. Remove the custard toasts when done, dust with powdered sugar, and garnish with chopped mint. Repeat the cooking process with the remaining brioche slices.
8. Serve warm.

Frozen Pretzel In The Air Fryer
Servings: 2
Cooking Time: 5 Minutes

Ingredients:
- 2 frozen soft pretzels, plus the salt from the box.
- 1 tablespoon water

Directions:
1. Place 2 frozen pretzels in the air fryer basket.
2. Lightly brush the tops of the pretzels with water and sprinkle on salt that came in the package, if desired.
3. Air fry at 320 degrees F for 3-5 minutes or until cooked through. Serve warm.
NOTES
HOW TO REHEAT PRETZELS:
Place pretzels in your air fryer basket.
Heat at 320 degrees for 2-3 minutes or until hot and crispy.

Hash Browns In The Air Fryer

Servings: 4
Cooking Time: 23 Minutes

Ingredients:
- 16 oz frozen shredded hash brown potatoes
- ½ teaspoon garlic powder
- Kosher salt, to taste
- Black pepper, to taste

Directions:
1. Preheat your air fryer to 370 degrees F.
2. Spread the frozen hash browns in a single layer inside, spray the top of the hash brown layer with olive oil spray, then sprinkle with garlic powder, salt, and pepper to taste.
3. Cook for 18 minutes. Use a spatula to divide the hash browns and carefully flip them. Spray with olive oil spray and continue to air fry for about 5 more minutes, or until they're golden brown and crispy to your liking.
4. Remove to a serving plate, season with additional salt and pepper if desired, and serve.
NOTES
HOW TO REHEAT HASH BROWNS IN THE AIR FRYER:
Preheat your air fryer to 370 degrees.
Place the leftover shredded hash browns in the air fryer and cook for 3 to 5 minutes, until warmed and crisped thoroughly.

Air Fryer Butternut Squash

Servings: 2
Cooking Time: 15 Minutes

Ingredients:
- 1 small butternut squash 1" dice (4-5 cups)
- 2 tablespoon olive oil
- 1 tablespoon brown sugar
- ¼ teaspoon cinnamon
- salt and pepper to taste

Directions:
1. Preheat air fryer to 400°F.
2. Peel the squash and scoop seeds out with a spoon, chop squash into 1 inch pieces.
3. Toss squash with oil and seasonings and place in the air fryer basket.
4. Cook for 12-15 minutes or until squash is tender.

Air Fried Italian Breaded Eggplant

Ingredients:
- 1 medium eggplant
- 1 tsp. salt
- 1/2 cup all-purpose flour
- 2 eggs
- 1 cup Italian breadcrumbs
- 1/4 cup olive oil
- 1 lb. fresh mozzarella cheese, sliced into rounds
- 1 jar spaghetti sauce

Directions:
1. Slice eggplant into disks
2. Place eggplant disks on paper towels to dry. Sprinkle salt on both sides and wait about 20 minutes
3. Take out 3 bowls. In the first bowl, add the flour
4. In the second bowl, mix together breadcrumbs and olive oil
5. In the third bow, beat 2 eggs
6. Coat each disk in flour, eggs, and breadcrumbs
7. Place in air fryer and cook at 390F for 8-11 minutes
8. Coat each eggplant with sauce and mozzarella cheese
9. Place basket back in air fryer and cook at 350F for 3-5 minutes
10. Enjoy!

Pumpkin Bread Pudding

Servings: 5

Ingredients:
- 1 cup milk
- 1 cup pumpkin puree
- 1 teaspoon vanilla
- ¼ teaspoon kosher salt
- ½ cup brown sugar
- 3 tablespoons granulated sugar
- 1 teaspoon nutmeg
- ½ teaspoon allspice
- ½ teaspoon cinnamon
- ¼ teaspoon ground cloves
- 2 eggs, beaten
- ½ loaf of bread (340 grams), cut into 2-inch cubes
- ½ cup dried cranberries
- ½ cup pecans
- Powdered15 sugar, for garnish (optional)
- Items Needed:
- Kitchen scale (optional, for bread)

Directions:
1. Whisk the milk, pumpkin puree, vanilla, salt, both sugars, and all spices together in a large bowl until smooth.
2. Add in the eggs and whisk until fully incorporated.
3. Add the cubed bread to the mixture and let soak for 15 minutes. Then, stir in the dried cranberries and pecans.
4. Line the inner Air Fryer basket with parchment paper, being sure to cover all the sides of the basket.
5. Place the bread pudding into the air fryer basket.
6. Select the Bake function, adjust temperature to 320°F and time to 25 minutes, press Shake, then press Start/Pause.
7. Cover the bread pudding with foil halfway through cooking. The Shake Reminder will let you know when.
8. Remove the air fryer basket and let cool for 5 minutes before removing the bread pudding and transferring it to a serving dish.
9. Serve warm, garnished with powdered sugar if desired.

Bacon & Pepper Breakfast Hash

Servings: 4
Cooking Time: 45 Minutes

Ingredients:
- 225g uncooked streaky bacon, cut in 1cm pieces
- 1 small onion, peeled, diced
- 1 red bell pepper, diced
- 2 white potatoes, peeled, diced
- 1 teaspoon paprika
- 1 teaspoon ground black pepper, plus more for seasoning
- 1 teaspoon celery or garlic salt
- 1 teaspoon sea salt, plus more for seasoning
- 4 eggs
- COOKING MODE
- When entering cooking mode - We will enable your screen to stay 'always on' to avoid any unnecessary interruptions whilst you cook!

Directions:
1. Remove the crisper plate from the pan and insert pan in unit. Preheat the unit by selecting ROAST, setting the temperature to 180°C and setting the time to 3 minutes. Select START/ STOP to begin.
2. After 3 minutes, add bacon to the pan. Reinsert pan. Select ROAST, set temperature to 180°C and set time to 45 minutes. Select START/STOP to begin. Cook for 5 minutes, or until bacon is crispy, stirring occasionally.
3. After 5 minutes, remove pan from unit and add the onion, pepper, potatoes and spices. Stir to incorporate. Reinsert pan to resume cooking.
4. Cook for 35 minutes, stirring occasionally, until potatoes are cooked through and golden brown.
5. Once vegetables are browned, remove pan from unit and crack four eggs onto the surface of the hash. Season with additional salt and pepper to taste. Reinsert pan to resume cooking.
6. Cook for 3 to 5 minutes, or until eggs are cooked to your preference. Serve immediately.

Nut-free Granola

Servings: 12
Cooking Time: 20 Minutes

Ingredients:

- Dry Ingredients:
- 2 cups (220 g) rolled oats gluten-free if needed
- ½ cup (70 g) sunflower seeds (see notes)
- ½ heaped cup (50 g) shredded unsweetened coconut (see notes)
- ½ tsp cinnamon
- ⅓ tsp sea salt
- ⅓ tsp cardamom (optional)
- ¼ tsp ground ginger
- Wet Ingredients:
- 1 cup dried fruit (see notes)
- ¼ cup + 1 Tbsp (100 g) maple syrup (see notes)
- ¼ cup (60 g) sunflower seed butter (see notes)
- ½ tsp vanilla extract

Directions:

1. You can watch the video in the post for visual instructions.
2. Line a large baking sheet with parchment paper and preheat the oven to 325 degrees Fahrenheit (165 degrees Celsius).
3. Add all dry ingredients into a big bowl and stir with a spoon.
4. Next, add dried fruit of choice (check the recipe notes below for options), maple syrup, sunflower seed butter, and vanilla extract. Stir with a spoon until all dry ingredients are coated and everything is well mixed.
5. Transfer the mixture onto the lined baking sheet and spread it out evenly.
6. Bake in the oven for about 20 minutes, stirring halfway through. Then gently press the stirred granola down with a wooden spoon (or spatula) so that it sticks together.
7. Check after 16-18 minutes if the granola is already lightly brown. Watch it closely, to avoid burning. Remove the baking sheet from the oven.
8. Let it cool completely without touching it. Once it gets cooler, the granola will crisp up. Store in air-tight containers.
9. Enjoy your homemade nut-free granola with plant-based milk, or use it to make these delicious GRANOLA CUPS.

Notes

You can use pepitas (pumpkin seeds) if you are allergic to coconut.

You can use nuts of choice (if not nut-free) instead of sunflower seeds.

Dried fruit: I used 1/4 cup raisins, 1/4 cup chopped apricots, 1/4 cup white mulberries, 1/4 cup dried goji berries. Feel free to use any dried fruit of choice, e.g. cranberries, chopped dates, mango, etc.

You can use agave syrup or rice malt syrup instead of maple syrup.

You can use nut butter of choice (e.g. cashew butter, coconut butter, almond butter, etc.) if not nut-free.

If you love granola, you might also love these Chocolate Granola Bars.

The recipe makes 12 servings (1/3 cup each). Nutrition facts are for one serving.

Check the blog post for the air fryer method.

Air Fryer Cauliflower Tacos

Servings: 12
Cooking Time: 15 Minutes

Ingredients:

- 2 eggs
- 2 t chili powder
- 1 t cumin
- 1 cup panko bread crumbs I used a gluten-free kind
- 1 head cauliflower cut into bite sized florets
- oil spray - as needed
- 12 tortillas I used all corn
- Mango Salsa optional topping
- diced cabbage optional topping

Directions:

1. In a bowl, whisk together the eggs and spices.
2. In another shallow bowl, put your bread crumbs.
3. Dredge one cauliflower floret at a time through the egg mixture and then into the bread crumbs. Once floret is fully covered

place into air fryer basket. Be sure to put the vegetables in a single layer and not to over crowd within the basket.

4.   Give the cauliflower florets a spritz of oil, if you wish. This will help the breading to crisp up. This step is optional.

5.   Air fry the cauliflower bites at 350 degrees F for 14 minutes. At the 7 minute mark (half way through the cooking process) remove the air fryer basket and gently shake the veggie pieces.

6.   When air fryer timer goes off, you can construct your tacos. Equally divide the air fried cauliflower pieces onto the 12 warmed tortillas. Top with your favorite toppings: I prefer diced purple cabbage and mango salsa.

7.   ENJOY!

Notes

Tips for Air Fryer Tacos

If you aren't a cauliflower fan, you can sub in another vegetable like zucchini planks.

You can make this recipe vegan by subbing OUT the two eggs and replacing then with ¼ cup of maple syrup.

This recipe does reheat well. Just reheat your cauliflower bites first, then your tortilla.

If you do not have bread crumbs, you can always smash/crumble some crackers or even a Chex style cereal.

Air Fryer Zucchini Fritters

Servings: 4
Cooking Time: 10 Minutes

Ingredients:

- 1 medium zucchini 8 oz
- ½ teaspoon salt or to taste
- 1 egg
- ¼ cup seasoned bread crumbs
- 1 tablespoon flour
- ½ teaspoon baking powder
- ⅓ cup cheddar cheese
- 1 tablespoon parmesan cheese
- ½ teaspoon Italian seasoning
- 1 green onion thinly sliced
- cooking spray

Directions:

1.   Shred zucchini using a box grater. Toss shredded zucchini with 1/2 teaspoon salt and let sit in a strainer 5-10 minutes.

2.   Using cheesecloth or a tea towel, squeeze out as much liquid from the zucchini as possible.

3.   Combine all ingredients in a bowl and form into 4 patties, approximately 3" across.

4.   Preheat air fryer to 370°F.

5.   Spray each side of the fritters with cooking spray and place in the air fryer.

6.   Cook 12-14 minutes or until crisp on the outside and tender inside.

Antipasto Egg Rolls

Servings: 12

Ingredients:

- 12 egg roll wrappers
- 12 slices provolone
- 12 slices deli ham
- 36 slices pepperoni
- 1 c. shredded mozzarella
- 1 c. sliced pepperoncini
- Vegetable oil, for frying on stovetop
- 1/4 c. freshly grated Parmesan
- Italian dressing, for serving

Directions:

1.   FOR STOVETOP

2.   Place an egg roll wrapper on a clean surface in a diamond shape place a slice of provolone in the center. Top with one slice of ham, 3 slices of pepperoni, and a large pinch of both mozzarella and pepperoncini. Fold up bottom half and tightly fold in sides. Gently roll, then seal fold with a couple drops of water.

3.   In a large skillet over medium heat, heat oil (it should reach 1" up the side of pan) until it pops and bubbles when a drop of water is added to the pan. Add egg rolls and fry until golden, 1 minute per side, then transfer to a paper towel-lined plate.

4.   Garnish with Parmesan and parsley and serve immediately, with Italian dressing on the side for dipping.

5.   FOR AIR FRYER

6.   Place an egg roll wrapper on a clean surface in a diamond shape place a slice of

provolone in the center. Top with one slice of ham, 3 slices of pepperoni, and a large pinch of both mozzarella and pepperoncini. Fold up bottom half and tightly fold in sides. Gently roll, then seal fold with a couple drops of water.
7. Working in batches, cook egg rolls at 390° until golden, about 12 minutes, flipping halfway through.

Air Fryer Jalapeno Popper Egg Rolls
Servings: 4
Cooking Time: 8 Minutes

Ingredients:
- 8 egg roll wrappers
- 8 ounces cream cheese softened
- 2 jalapenos medium and chopped
- 2 bacon slices crumbled

Directions:
1. In a medium mixing bowl, add the cream cheese, chopped jalapenos, and bacon slices. Stir together to combine.
2. Lay out wrappers with corners left and right. Spoon mixture into the center of the wonton.
3. Fold bottom corn over the filling and tuck under. Next, fold in the left and right corners, and then turn over, to make a large pillow shape.
4. Lightly spray the air fryer basket, and place each Egg Roll in the basket without stacking or overlapping. Lightly spray each egg roll to help with crispness and color.
5. Air fry at 400 degrees F for 8-10 minutes, until golden and crispy. Turn halfway during the air frying process.
NOTES
Variations
Add seasonings - If you want to add a little bit of garlic powder, onion powder, soy sauce, or any other flavors, go for it!
Add varied ingredients - When making this perfect appetizer, you can add other ingredients to the spring roll wrappers. You just need to make sure that you don't overfill, otherwise, the edges of the wrapper won't seal.

Add some mozzarella cheese, cheddar cheese, diced green onions, bacon bits, or anything else that would change up the flavor.

Air Fryer Hard-boiled Eggs Recipe
Servings: 12
Cooking Time: 15 Minutes

Ingredients:
- 12 large eggs

Directions:
1. Heat an air fryer to 270°F. Place 12 eggs in the air fryer basket in one layer. Air fry for 15 minutes.
2. Almost immediately after the eggs are ready, peel them under a gentle stream of cold water.
RECIPE NOTES
Storage: The peeled eggs can be refrigerated in an airtight container for up to 4 days.

Air Fryer Eggplant Parmesan
Servings: 6
Cooking Time: 11 Minutes

Ingredients:
- 1 large eggplant or two small
- 1 teaspoon salt
- ⅔ cup seasoned bread crumbs
- 2 tablespoons parmesan cheese grated
- 1 teaspoon Italian seasoning
- ¼ teaspoon garlic powder
- 2 eggs whisked
- ¼ cup flour
- 1 cup marinara sauce
- 1 cup mozzarella cheese shredded

Directions:
1. Preheat the air fryer to 380°F.
2. Slice eggplant into ⅓" slices and pat dry.
3. Combine bread crumbs, parmesan cheese, Italian seasoning, salt, and garlic powder in a medium bowl.
4. Place whisked eggs in another bowl and flour in another.
5. Dip each eggplant slice into the flour, then into the egg and finally into the bread crumb

mixture. Spray each side of the eggplant with cooking spray.

6. Place in a single layer in the air fryer and cook 5 minutes. Flip over and cook for 4 minutes or until crispy and golden brown.

7. Add marinara sauce and mozzarella cheese on top and cook for another 2-3 minutes or until cheese is melted.

Notes

To remove excess moisture from eggplant slices, sprinkle a little salt on each slice and wipe off after 5 minutes. This helps to make them extra crispy!

Gently press the breadcrumb coating into the eggplant slices to help it adhere to the eggplant before air frying.

Air Fryer French Toast Sticks
Servings: 4
Cooking Time: 8 Minutes

Ingredients:
- 8 slices Italian style bread thickly sliced
- 3 eggs
- 1 cup milk
- 1 tablespoon sugar
- 1 teaspoon vanilla
- ½ teaspoon cinnamon

Directions:
1. Preheat air fryer to 350°F. Spray basket with pan release.
2. Whisk eggs, milk, sugar, vanilla, and cinnamon in a shallow bowl or dish.
3. Cut bread into 1" sticks - roughly 4 sticks per slice of bread.
4. Dip sticks into the egg mixture allowing a few seconds for the egg to soak into the bread.
5. Place the sticks in two rows in the air fryer basket and cook for 4 minutes.
6. After 4 minutes, flip the sticks over and cook for an additional 4 or until they are golden in color.

Air Fryer Hard Boiled Eggs
Servings: 4
Cooking Time: 18 Minutes

Ingredients:
- 8 large eggs

Directions:
1. Preheat air fryer to 250°F.
2. Add eggs in a single layer in the air fryer basket.
3. For hard-cooked eggs cook for 16-18 minutes. Once cooked place in an ice bath until cool.
4. Peel under cool running water.

Notes

You can cook as many eggs at one time as you need.

Eggs are cooked directly from the fridge (cold). If your eggs are room temperature, you may need to adjust cooking time.

These were tested in both a Vortex Air Fryer and two different Cosori Air Fryers. Other brands may vary by a minute or two and it may take a couple of batches to learn your machine. Cook just one or two eggs at first to be certain they're cooked how you like them.

Air Fryer Egg Cooking times

Soft: Cook 11-12 minutes

Medium: Cook 13-14 minutes

Hard: Cook 16-18 minutes

Air Fryer Stuffed Spaghetti Squash
Servings: 4
Cooking Time: 45 Minutes

Ingredients:
- 1 medium spaghetti squash 3 lbs
- 1 pound lean ground beef
- 1 small onion diced
- 2 cloves garlic minced
- 24 ounces marinara sauce or pasta sauce
- 1 teaspoon Italian seasoning
- 1 cup cheese + extra for topping mozzarella or cheddar, shredded
- ½ cup parmesan cheese shredded
- salt & pepper to taste

Directions:

1. Preheat the air fryer to 370°F. Slice the spaghetti squash in half, scoop out the seeds and discard.
2. Cook Spaghetti Squash
3. Brush the squash with olive oil and place in the air fryer cut side up and cook for 25-30 minutes or until fork tender.
4. Once the squash is cooked, gently scrape the insides into a large bowl and set it aside. Reserve the shells for filling.
5. Prepare Sauce
6. Increase the temperature of the Air Fryer to 380°F.
7. Mix ground beef, diced onion, and minced garlic in a bowl. *see note Place the beef mixture in the air fryer basket and use a spoon to spread it out a little bit. Cook for 5 minutes and use a spoon to break up the meat. Cook for an additional 5 minutes until the beef is browned and no pink remains. Drain any fat.
8. Combine the marinara sauce with the ground beef and Italian seasoning in an air fryer safe pan or bowl. Return to the air fryer and cook for 10 minutes or until bubbly.
9. Assembly
10. While the sauce is cooking combine the cheese with the cooked spaghetti squash and place it back into the squash shell.
11. Top with the ground beef mixture. Top with extra shredded cheese.
12. Place the squash back into the air fryer and cook for 7-9 minutes or until the cheese is melted.
Notes
To make it easy to cut spaghetti squash, poke it with a fork a few times and microwave for 3-4 minutes.
Option: If preferred the ground beef mixture and the sauce can be prepared on the stovetop while the squash is roasting in the air fryer.
Brown the beef, onion and garlic in a pan. Drain fat.
Add sauce ingredients and simmer 5 minutes.
Ensure your bowl or container for the sauce is air fryer safe.
Leftover spaghetti sauce or meat sauce can be used in place of the home-made sauce.

Air Fryer Crescent Rolls
Servings: 8
Cooking Time: 6 Minutes

Ingredients:
- 1 package of refrigerated crescent rolls
- OPTIONAL
- Butter
- Jam or Jelly

Directions:
1. Preheat your air fryer to 350 degrees.
2. On a parchment paper or mat, roll your crescent rolls, from the wide end down to the point. Then slightly curl the ends of the dough to a crescent shape. Lay them on the mat.
3. Once your air fryer is preheated, lay your mat of croissants into the basket. Cook for 5-7 minutes, checking at the 4-minute mark. They will be golden brown on the tops and the bottoms firm.*
NOTES
*Optional: you could brush them with melted butter once cooked or just serve with butter and jam.

Air Fryer French Toast
Servings: 4
Cooking Time: 5 Minutes

Ingredients:
- 4 slices white bread
- 2 large eggs
- 3/4 cup milk
- 1 tablespoon sugar
- 1/2 teaspoon vanilla extract
- 1/4 teaspoon cinnamon

Directions:
1. Whisk together the eggs, milk, sugar, vanilla extract, and sugar.
2. Add the bread slices, one at a time, and soak for 10 seconds, flip, and soak for another 10 seconds.
3. Grease an air fryer basket and place the french toast in one slice at a time, air fry at 180C/350F for 5-7 minutes, flipping halfway through.

4. Repeat the process until all the bread is cooked.

Notes

TO STORE: Put the leftovers in an airtight container and store them in the refrigerator for 2-3 days.

TO FREEZE: You can keep the leftovers in the freezer for up to 2 months by putting them in freezer-safe bags or containers.

TO REHEAT: Place slices of the French toast in a toaster or toaster oven and heat up until warm.

Air Fryer Rusks, With Buttermilk & Muesli

Servings: 16
Cooking Time: 50 Minutes

Ingredients:
- 500g self-raising flour
- 100g sugar
- Pinch sea salt
- 150g butter, cold & cubed
- 250g buttermilk, room temperature
- 1 large egg
- 140g muesli

Directions:
1. Lightly grease a 20 x 20cm baking tin.
2. In a large bowl whisk together the self-raising flour, sugar and salt.
3. Add the butter and work it into the dry ingredients until the mixture resembles wet sand.
4. Whisk the buttermilk and egg together well.
5. Add the buttermilk mixture and the muesli into the dry ingredients.
6. Mix everything together.
7. Divide the dough into 16 balls and shape them into little logs.
8. Arrange them side by side in the baking tin.
9. Place the tin in the Vortex Plus basket and select Air Fry at 160°C for 40 minutes.
10. Remove the baked rusks from the tin and return them, whole, upside down to the air fryer basket. Air Fry at 160°C again for 5 minutes.
11. Break the rusks apart into individuals and place them in the basket.
12. Dehydrate the rusks at 79°C for 4 hours until hard.
13. Keep rusks in a sealed container and enjoy dunking into your favourite hot beverage!

Air Fryer Poached Egg Avocado Smash Toast

Servings: 2

Ingredients:
- 2 thin slices whole wheat bread
- 1 large avocado
- 1 tbsp. fresh lemon juice
- 2 tsp. chopped fresh basil leaves, plus torn leaves for serving
- Kosher salt
- Olive oil cooking spray
- 4 tsp. lukewarm water
- 2 large eggs
- 1/2 c. cherry or grape tomatoes, halved
- Crushed red pepper flakes (optional)

Directions:
1. Working in batches if necessary, in an air-fryer basket, arrange bread in a single layer. Cook at 350°, flipping halfway through, until light golden, 3 to 4 minutes. Transfer toast to plates.
2. Using a spoon, scoop avocado flesh into a medium bowl. Add lemon juice, chopped basil, and a pinch of salt. Mash with a fork until combined yet still chunky; season with salt, if desired.
3. Lightly coat 2 (4-oz.) ramekins with cooking spray. Fill each with 2 teaspoons water. Crack 1 egg into each.
4. Place ramekins in air-fryer basket. Cook at 350° until egg whites are set and yolks are still runny, 6 to 8 minutes.
5. Spread avocado mixture over toasts. Carefully remove ramekins from air-fryer basket one at a time (they will be hot). Run a spatula around edges of eggs, then slide onto avocado mixture, flipping eggs upside down

(so bottom of egg in ramekin is face up on plate).
6. Top toast with tomatoes; season with a pinch of salt. Garnish with torn basil and red pepper flakes, if using.

Air Fryer Cinnamon Roll Bites
Servings: 8

Ingredients:
- 1 can (12.4 oz) refrigerated Pillsbury™ Cinnamon Rolls with Original Icing (8 Count)
- 1/3 cup granulated sugar
- 1/2 teaspoon ground cinnamon
- Dipping Icing
- 4 oz (half of 8-oz package) cream cheese, softened
- 1 tablespoon butter, softened
- 1 cup powdered sugar
- 2 to 3 teaspoons milk

Directions:
1. Cut 8-inch round of cooking parchment paper. Place in bottom of air fryer basket.
2. Separate dough into 8 rolls. Cut each roll into 4 equal pieces; place 16 pieces in bottom of air fryer basket. Set icing aside.
3. Set air fryer to 325°F; cook 3 minutes. With tongs, turn over each piece; cook 2 to 3 minutes or until golden brown. Remove from air fryer. Repeat with remaining 16 pieces.
4. Meanwhile, in large resealable food-storage plastic bag, mix cinnamon and granulated sugar. In small bowl, beat cream cheese and softened butter with electric mixer on medium speed until smooth. Beat in powdered sugar, reserved icing and enough milk for dipping consistency.
5. Shake warm bites in cinnamon-sugar. Serve warm with dipping icing.

Air Fryer Bread
Servings: 1

Ingredients:
- Deselect All
- 2 tablespoons unsalted butter, melted, plus more for the pan
- 1 1/2 teaspoons active dry yeast
- 1 1/2 teaspoons sugar
- 1 1/2 teaspoons kosher salt
- 2 2/3 cups all-purpose flour (see Cook's Note)

Directions:
1. Butter a 6-by-3-inch round pan and set aside.
2. Combine the butter, yeast, sugar, salt and 1 cup warm water in a stand mixer fitted with the dough hook attachment. With the mixer on low speed, add 1/2 cup of the flour at a time, waiting for each addition to be fully incorporated before adding more. Once all of the flour is added, knead on medium speed for 8 minutes.
3. Transfer the dough to the prepared pan, cover and let rise until doubled in size, about 1 hour.
4. Add the pan with the dough to a 3.5-quart air fryer and set to 380 degrees F. Cook until the bread is dark brown and the internal temperature registers 200 degrees F, about 20 minutes. Let cool in the pan 5 minutes, then turn out onto a rack to cool completely.
5. Cook's Note
6. When measuring flour, we spoon it into a dry measuring cup and level off excess. (Scooping directly from the bag compacts the flour, resulting in dry baked goods.)

POULTRY RECIPES

Chicken Tempura
Servings: 4
Cooking Time: 4 Minutes

Ingredients:
- For the chicken
- 1 lb chicken breast sliced into strips
- 3 tablespoons soy sauce
- 1/2 teaspoon salt
- 1/2 teaspoon pepper
- 1 cup vegetable oil
- For the batter
- 3/4 cup all purpose flour
- 1/4 cup cornstarch
- 1/4 teaspoon baking soda
- 1 large egg whisked
- 1 cup soda water seltzer/sparkling water

Directions:
1. In a mixing bowl, add the chicken breast, soy sauce, salt and pepper.
2. In a separate bowl, add the flour, cornstarch, and baking soda and mix well. Make a well in the center and add the egg and soda water. Gently mix until combined.
3. Add the oil to a deep pot or saucepan and place it over medium heat.
4. Moving quickly, dip the chicken in the batter until fully coated. Shake off excess batter.
5. Place several chicken pieces in the hot oil and fry for 2-3 minutes until golden. Remove the cooked chicken and place them on a paper towel to soak up excess oil. Repeat the process until all the chicken is cooked.
Notes
Air fryer and oven instructions in the body of the post.
TO STORE: Leftovers can be stored in the refrigerator, covered, for up to five days.
TO FREEZE: Place the cooked and cooled tempura in an airtight container and store it in the freezer for up to 6 months.
TO REHEAT: Either reheat tempura in a non-stick pan or in the air fryer/oven. Do not microwave them as they will be soggy.

Air Fryer Crispy Red-pepper-jelly Wings
Servings: 2-3
Cooking Time: 25 Minutes

Ingredients:
- 2 tablespoons olive oil
- 2 tablespoons honey
- 1/8 teaspoon cayenne pepper
- 1 tablespoon baking powder
- 1 tablespoon salt
- 1 pound chicken wings
- oil, for spraying
- 2 tablespoons butter, melted
- 1/4 cup Red Pepper Jelly

Directions:
1. In a large bowl, combine olive oil, honey, and cayenne pepper and set aside. In another large bowl, combine baking powder and salt. Add chicken wings and toss until well coated.
2. Place chicken wings in air fryer basket, spray with oil, set air fryer temperature to 200 degrees, and air fry for 15 minutes. After five minutes, turn wings, spray with oil, and continue cooking, shaking basket occasionally. Remove wings to reserved honey mixture and toss well to coat. Return wings to air fryer basket, set temperature to 400 degrees, and air fry for 10 minutes, shaking basket occasionally.
3. In a large bowl, combine melted butter and Red Pepper Jelly. Toss wings in jelly mixture and serve warm.
4. Cook's Note: One pound of chicken wings is about 10 to 12 wings, depending on the size of the wings.

Honey Sriracha Chicken
Servings: 6
Cooking Time: 1 Hour

Ingredients:
- CHICKEN:
- 1 4-lb Whole chicken

- 2 tsp Sea salt
- 1/2 tsp Black pepper
- 1/4 cup Honey (I used Wholesome Yum Keto Honey for sugar-free, but regular is fine if it fits your lifestyle)
- GARLIC SRIRACHA SAUCE:
- 4 cloves Garlic (minced)
- 1/4 cup Sriracha
- 2 tbsp Coconut aminos
- 2 tbsp Lemon juice
- 2 tbsp Olive oil
- 1 tsp Dried thyme
- 1 tsp Dried basil

Directions:
1. If you have time, remove the chicken from the fridge 30 minutes before cooking, which will help it cook more evenly.
2. Preheat the air fryer or oven to 350 degrees F (176 degrees C).
3. Season the chicken all over with salt and pepper, including inside the cavity.
4. In a small bowl, mix together the garlic, sriracha, coconut aminos, lemon juice, oil, thyme, and basil. Brush the chicken with the sauce, including underneath the skin and inside the cavity.
5. Air fryer cooking instructions: Place the chicken, back side up, into the air fryer basket. Air fry for 30 minutes. Flip the chicken so it's breast side up. Air fry for 20 more minutes. Remove the basket and brush the whole chicken with honey. Return to the air fryer and roast for 10-15 minutes, until a thermometer inserted in the thickest part of the breast reaches at least 160 degrees F (71 degrees C).
6. Oven cooking instructions: Place the chicken, back side up, into a roasting pan. Roast chicken in the oven for 45 minutes. Flip the chicken so it's breast side up. Roast for 30 more minutes. Remove the roasting pan and brush the whole chicken with honey. Return to the oven and roast for 15-20 minutes, until a thermometer inserted in the thickest part of the breast reaches at least 160 degrees F (71 degrees C).

7. Let the chicken rest for 10 minutes before carving. Internal temperature will rise about 5-10 degrees.
8. Serve honey sriracha chicken with the pan juice from the roasting pan or air fryer basket.

Gluten-free Air Fryer Fried Chicken
Servings: 4
Cooking Time: 25 Minutes

Ingredients:
- 1 1/3 cup buttermilk
- 1kg chicken, breast, legs and thighs, bone in, skin on
- 125g gluten-free plain flour
- 65g cornflour
- 1 tsp smoked paprika
- 1 tsp oregano
- 1/2 tsp chilli powder
- 1/2 tsp black pepper
- 2 tsp salt
- 1 tsp spray oil

Directions:
1. Mix the buttermilk and chicken in a bowl, cover with clingfilm and refrigerate for 1 hour.
2. Place the flour, cornflour, smoked paprika, oregano, chilli powder, black pepper and salt in a bowl and whisk to combine. Spread out on a plate. Take the chicken pieces, shake off excess buttermilk and dip into the coating, covering each side.
3. Place the chicken in the air fryer and cook at 200°C for for 22-25 minutes, turning halfway through, until crisp, golden and cooked through.

Air Fryer Chicken, Bacon And Creamed Corn Roll-ups

Servings: 2
Cooking Time: 20 Minutes

Ingredients:
- 1 chicken breast fillet
- 90g can creamed corn
- 60g cream cheese, chopped, at room temperature
- 40g (1/2 cup) pre-grated 3 cheese blend
- 1 tbsp chopped fresh coriander
- 4 streaky bacon rashers
- Tomato salsa, to serve
- Select all ingredients

Directions:
1. Use a long sharp knife to slice the chicken breast in half horizontally. Use a meat mallet to pound out the chicken breasts to about 5mm-thick.
2. Combine the corn, cream cheese, cheese blend and coriander in a bowl. Top one chicken piece with half the mixture. Top remaining chicken piece with remaining mixture. Carefully roll from the short end of the chicken to enclose. Wrap each piece of chicken in two pieces of bacon. Secure with toothpicks.
3. Spray the basket of the air fryer with oil. Place the chicken in the basket and air fry at 180C for 15 minutes, turning halfway through cooking, or until cooked through.
4. Discard toothpicks. Slice the chicken and serve with salsa.

Pickle Ham And Swiss Chicken Roll Ups

Servings: 4
Cooking Time: 25 Minutes

Ingredients:
- 4 1 lb thin boneless chicken cutlets
- 1 1/4 cups pickle juice (enough to cover chicken)
- 4 teaspoons deli mustard
- 2 oz thin sliced reduced sodium deli ham
- 2 oz shredded Swiss cheese
- 1-2 dill pickles (sliced very thin lengthwise, dried on paper towel (I used a mandolin))
- olive oil spray
- For the breading:
- 1 large egg (beaten)
- 1/3 cup seasoned wheat or gluten-free breadcrumbs*
- 1/3 cup seasoned wheat or gluten-free panko*
- cooking spray

Directions:
1. Oven Directions:
2. Place chicken in a shallow bowl and cover with pickle juice (enough to cover completely). Marinate in the refrigerator 8 hours.
3. After 8 hours, drain and dry the chicken completely on paper towels; discard marinade.
4. Preheat oven to 425F. Spray a baking sheet with oil.
5. Spread 1 teaspoon of mustard over each piece of chicken. Layer the ham on top, then the Swiss cheese and pickles along the center and roll.
6. Place egg in a medium bowl. In a shallow bowl, combine the bread crumbs and panko. Dip chicken in the egg wash, then into the breadcrumb mixture and shake off excess.
7. Transfer to the prepared baking sheet and spray the top generously with oil. Bake 25 minutes, until golden outside and cooked through.
8. Air Fryer Directions:
9. Follow steps 1-5.
10. Preheat the air fryer to 400F. Transfer to the air fryer basket in two batches until golden outside and cooked through in the center, about 12 minutes, turning half way.
Notes
*only 1/4 cup of each gets used in breading, so I subtracted what got thrown out from the macros.

Roast Chicken And Potatoes

Ingredients:
- Roast chicken:
- 1 small free-range chicken up to 1.3 – 1.5kg
- Zest of 1 ClemenGold (Clementine or orange)
- 200ml of freshly squeezed ClemenGold clementine juice (+-4) (or orange)
- 200ml strong chicken stock
- 3 cloves garlic, crushed
- 3cm piece of ginger, finely grated
- 4 sprigs of thyme
- Salt & pepper
- Drizzle of olive oil
- Roast potatoes with smoked paprika:
- 8 medium/small potatoes – aprox 700gms
- 2 Tbsp olive oil
- 1 tsp smoked paprika
- 1 tsp garlic powder
- Salt and pepper

Directions:
1. To make the roast chicken:
2. Add the zest, and juice of the clementine to a small jug with the chicken stock, garlic, and ginger.
3. Remove the drip tray from the air fryer basket and place the whole bird inside. Pour over the liquid and scatter the thyme stalks around.
4. Set the Vortex ClearCook Dual Air fryer to 'Roast' at 180C/350F for 1 hour.
5. Start with roasting the chicken with the breast facing up for 20 minutes. Then flip it so the underside faces up and browns (another 20 minutes), then turn it back to face up for the final 20 minutes. This way the chicken browns on all sides and doesn't overcook on one. You will be turning the chicken over twice during the hour cooking process.
6. Once cooked, remove, and set aside. Strain the pan juices and serve this as a delicious jus (light gravy) along with the chicken and roast potatoes.
7. To make the roast potatoes:

8. Slice the potatoes in half and add the olive oil and spices. Toss well to coat evenly. Tip this into the air fryer basket.
9. Set the Vortex ClearCook Dual Air fryer to 'Air Fry' at 190C/374F for 30 minutes.
10. Push the Sync Cook button and this new feature will ensure both the roast chicken and roast potatoes finish cooking at the same time! It's all about setting it and forgetting it. It does not matter that the food is pre-loaded. Just add the food once the air fryer has run its pre-heat cycle and reaches temp (it will prompt you!)
NOTES
Serve with a green vegetable on the side.

Air Fryer Chicken Tenders
Servings: 4-6

Ingredients:
- 2 lb. chicken tenders
- 1 c. buttermilk
- 1 1/2 tsp. seasoned salt, divided
- 3/4 tsp. black pepper, divided
- 1/2 c. all-purpose flour
- 2 eggs
- 2 c. panko breadcrumbs
- 1/2 c. freshly grated parmesan cheese (or 1/4 cup pre-grated parmesan cheese)
- Cooking spray, such as Pam Olive Oil
- Honey mustard, BBQ sauce, and/or ranch dressing, for serving

Directions:
1. In a zip-top plastic bag, combine the chicken tenders, buttermilk, 1 teaspoon of seasoned salt and ½ teaspoon of black pepper. Seal and massage the buttermilk mixture into the tenders. Let marinate for 30 minutes, or up to 2 hours, in the refrigerator.
2. Meanwhile, place the flour on a small plate. In a wide shallow bowl, whisk together the two eggs. In another wide, shallow bowl, combine the panko, parmesan cheese, remaining 1/2 teaspoon of seasoned salt and 1/4 teaspoon of black pepper.
3. Using a pair of tongs, remove the chicken from the buttermilk marinade (reserve the marinade) and place the chicken in a single

layer on a paper-towel lined plate. Pour the remaining buttermilk marinade into the bowl with the eggs and whisk to combine.

4. Working 2-3 tenders at a time, dredge all over in the flour, dip in the egg mixture to coat completely, then dredge to coat completely in the panko breadcrumb mixture. Repeat until all of the tenders are breaded. Spray all over both sides of each tender with cooking spray (olive oil spray gives great flavor!)

5. Working in two batches, place the tenders in a single layer, with about ½-inch of space between them. Cook in the air fryer set at 380°F for 8 minutes. Then flip and continue to cook for 4-6 minutes longer, until the internal temperature of the chicken reads 165°F. Repeat with the second batch of tenders. Serve immediately alongside dipping sauces such as honey mustard, BBQ sauce, and/or ranch dressing.

Notes

If you have the patience to wait and serve these all at once, hold the first batch of cooked tenders warm in a 200°F oven, until the second batch is finished.

Tandoori Style Chicken With A Raita Dip

Servings: 4

Ingredients:

- 640 g boneless chicken thighs, into chunks
- 400 ml natural yogurt
- 2 cm fresh ginger, grated
- 1 tsp cumin
- 1 tsp chilli powder
- 1 tsp lemon juice
- 1 tsp vegtable oil
- 1/2 cucumber, grated and squeezed of excess water
- 1 tbsp fresh mint leaves, finely chopped

Directions:

1. First marinade the chicken, in a bowl add 250mls of the yogurt, lemon juice, garlic, ginger and spices, and mix together.

2. Add the chicken pieces, and coat in the marinade – cover and keep in the fridge for at least an hour.

3. Make the raita – season the grated and squeezed cucumber with a little salt and mix into the rest of the yogurt with the mint.

4. Preheat the air fryer to 200 degrees, and lightly grease the basket with little oil cook the chicken for 15-20 mins – giving them a turn about half way through.

5. Serve up straight away with the raita.

Chicken Parm With Roasted Mediterranean Vegetables

Servings: 4

Ingredients:

- For the roasted vegetables
- 1 yellow pepper
- 1 red pepper
- 120g cherry tomatoes
- 1 courgette
- 1 red onion
- 120g button mushrooms
- 1 carrot
- salt
- pepper
- 1 tbsp oregano
- 2 tbsp olive oil
- For the chicken parm
- 1 chicken breast
- 100g plain flour
- 2 eggs
- 400g panko breadcrumbs
- 75g parmesan grated
- 100g tomato sauce
- 300g grated mozzarella
- COOKING MODE
- When entering cooking mode - We will enable your screen to stay 'always on' to avoid any unnecessary interruptions whilst you cook!

Directions:

1. Chop up the peppers, carrot, onion and courgette into roughly 2cm sized pieces

2. Cut the mushrooms in half and add all vegetables into a mixing bowl

3. Add the olive oil, salt, pepper and oregano and toss until evenly coated

4. Butterfly the chicken breasts into two equally sized halves

5. Mix together the panko breadcrumbs and parmesan in a shallow tray

6. Crack the eggs into a bowl and whisk

7. Pour the flour into a bowl

8. One-by-one, coat each chicken piece in flour, then coat in the egg mixture, before pressing firmly into the breadcrumbs

9. Dip back into the egg, before a final coat of breadcrumbs to ensure an even coating

10. Add the vegetables into one side of the air fryer, and the chicken parm into the other

11. Select AIR FRY

12. Set the vegetables at 180C for 20 minutes (shake halfway through cooking), and the chicken at 170C for 10 minutes (flip halfway through cooking)

13. Select SYNC and press the dial to begin cooking

14. After 10 minutes, add cherry tomatoes to the vegetables (shake halfway through cooking).

15. When the chicken is done, place on a sheet of baking paper. Smother in tomato sauce and cover with mozzarella. Whilst plating your vegetables, cook the chicken for a further 3 minutes until the cheese is bubbling.

16. Serve and enjoy!

Air Fryer Turkey Bacon
Servings: 5
Cooking Time: 10 Minutes

Ingredients:
- 10 slices Turkey Bacon

Directions:
1. Preheat air fryer to 350 degrees Fahrenheit. Place the bacon slices flat in the basket of the air fryer in a single layer.

2. Air Fry at 350 degrees Fahrenheit for 8-10 minutes, flip bacon halfway through the cooking process. Check the bacon after 10 minutes for crispiness. For crispier bacon, add another 1-2 minutes cook time.

3. Remove bacon from air fryer, then place the bacon on paper towel to cool. Repeat until all slices of bacon are cooked.

NOTES
Exact time may vary depending on the type of air fryer and brands of bacon used.

Slow Cooker Chicken Taco Salad
Servings: 6
Cooking Time: 6 Hrs

Ingredients:
- FOR THE CHICKEN
- 2 pounds chicken , preferrably boneless and skinless (*see head note)
- 1 cup tomato sauce or salsa
- 2 Tablespoons Worcestershire sauce or soy sauce
- 1 Tablespoon chili powder
- 1 teaspoon ground cumin
- 1 teaspoon onion powder
- 1 teaspoon garlic powder
- 1/2 teaspoon salt , or more to taste
- Fresh cracked black pepper , to taste
- 1/2 teaspoon chipotle powder , or to taste (optional, for spicy flavor)
- FOR THE SALAD
- 6 cups chopped lettuce
- OPTIONAL TOPPINGS:
- salsa
- gaucamole
- sour cream
- cheese
- sliced avocado
- lime wedges
- hot sauce
- sliced radishes
- diced or sliced red onion
- EQUIPMENT
- Slow Cooker

Directions:
1. Add all the ingredients into the slow cooker (chicken, tomato sauce or salsa, Worcestershire sauce, chili powder, cumin, onion powder, garlic powder, salt & pepper, and optional chipotle powder). Stir to

completely coat the chicken with the spices & sauce.

2. Slow cook 6-8 hours on low or 4-5 hours on high.

3. Take the chicken pieces out of the slow cooker, cut into 1-2 inch pieces, then place back in the slow cooker. Shed with a couple forks to break up the chicken.

4. Taste the chicken and add more salt if needed.

5. When ready to serve, top the lettuce with the shredded chicken and with whatever other preferred toppings you like.

Buffalo Ranch Chicken Dip

Servings: 12
Cooking Time: 30 Minutes

Ingredients:

- 8 ounces cream cheese softened
- ½ cup sour cream
- ½ cup ranch dressing
- 2 green onions thinly sliced
- 2 cups shredded chicken cooked
- 1 cup buffalo sauce divided
- 1 cup pepper jack cheese shredded
- 1 cup cheddar cheese shredded

Directions:

1. Preheat oven to 375°F.

2. Combine cream cheese, sour cream, ranch dressing, ½ cup of the buffalo sauce, and green onions with a mixer on medium speed. Spread in a a pie plate or small casserole dish (2qt).

3. Place chicken over the cream cheese mixture and drizzle with the remaining ½ cup buffalo sauce.

4. Top with cheeses and bake 20-25 minutes or until hot & bubbly. Let cool 5 minutes before serving.

Notes

Ranch dressing can be substituted with additional sour cream and ranch dressing mix. A hand mixer makes a fluffier dip that is easier to scoop but this can be mixed with a spoon if preferred.

Serve with crostini, tortilla chips, soft pretzels, or celery sticks for dipping.

Air Fryer Grilled Chicken Breast

Servings: 3
Cooking Time: 20 Minutes

Ingredients:

- 3 chicken breasts boneless, skinless
- 1 Tablespoon olive oil
- 1/2 teaspoon ground black pepper
- 1/2 teaspoon onion powder
- 1/2 teaspoon garlic powder
- 1/4 teaspoon rosemary dried
- 1/4 teaspoon sea salt

Directions:

1. Rinse and use a paper towel to pat dry the chicken breasts.

2. Add the chicken breasts to a large resealable bag.

3. Add the olive oil and seasonings to the bag with the chicken breasts. Seal and gently toss the bag to coat the chicken evenly with the olive oil and seasonings.

4. Coat the basket of the air fryer with cooking spray or parchment paper if needed.

5. Place the seasoned chicken breasts into the air fryer basket in a single layer.

6. Air fry the chicken breasts at 390 degrees Fahrenheit for 20 minutes, flipping the chicken breasts halfway through the cooking time.

7. Use a digital meat thermometer and make sure the chicken has reached an internal temperature of 165 degrees Fahrenheit.

8. Carefully remove the chicken from the air fryer and serve.

NOTES

I love to meal prep with air fryer grilled chicken. I slice the cooked chicken breasts and add them to an airtight container with cooked rice and seasoned and cooked broccoli. You can also consider serving this with sweet potatoes, potato salad, wedge salad, or fries.

The sky is the limit when it comes to seasoning chicken. I love to use rosemary, chili powder, Italian seasoning, brown sugar, lemon pepper with a little lemon juice, and even top the finishe product with BBQ sauce. There are many different options, so you can easily change this recipe up often.

Store leftover grilled chicken breast in an airtight container in the refrigerator for up to 3 days.

Japanese Style Fried Chicken Recipe

Ingredients:
- 6 cream crackers
- 1 skinless chicken breast fillet
- 1 garlic clove, crushed
- 1 medium egg
- 1 tbsp butter
- 1 tbsp dry parsley
- Plain flour
- ½ lemon
- Salt and pepper, to taste

Directions:
1. Add the garlic and zest of the lemon to a food processor along with the butter, parsley, salt, pepper and crackers. Process until the mixture is very fine.
2. Sprinkle the flour onto a second plate, then crack the eggs into a small bowl to beat with a fork.
3. Cut the chicken breast into 2cm pieces, then roll the chicken pieces in the flour until all sides are completely coated then dip them into the egg, and finally the crumbs.
4. Spray the chicken on all sides with oil and place them into a 200°C air fryer and cook for 10-15 minutes until the chicken is golden and crisp.
5. Top Tip! Best served with fluffy rice, stir-fried noodles or steamed vegetables.

Air Fryer Sweet And Sour Chicken
Servings: 4
Cooking Time: 18 Minutes

Ingredients:
- 1 pound chicken cut into strips or small pieces
- 1/4 cup cornstarch
- Sweet and Sour Sauce Ingredients:
- 1/2 cup sugar
- 1/4 cup white wine vinegar
- 1 tablespoon soy sauce
- 1 teaspoon garlic minced
- 1/4 cup pineapple juice
- 1/4 cup water
- 2 tablespoon cornstarch

Directions:
1. Cut the chicken into cubed chunks, then toss in a large bowl with cornstarch and coat the chicken evenly. Preheat the Air Fryer to 380° Fahrenheit.
2. To prepare the basket, use a cooking spray and lightly cover the bottom of air fryer basket. Then lay the chicken in a single layer and be sure not to stack chicken or overcrowd the basket.
3. Spritz coated chicken with a light mist of olive oil spray. Air fry at 380 degrees F for 14-18 minutes. Turn chicken pieces over halfway through cooking time.
4. While the chicken is cooking, add the sugar, white wine vinegar, soy sauce, and garlic, and pineapple juice into a small saucepan and whisk over medium heat until the sauce reaches a small boil.
5. Once the sugar has completely dissolved in the mix, combine the cornstarch and water, then add to the sauce. Keep stirring on heat for about 10-15 seconds, then remove from heat. Allow the sauce to thicken for around 5 minutes. Continue to whisk.
6. Drizzle sauce over chicken or toss in a large bowl to coat each piece. Garnish with green onions and sesame seeds if desired.
NOTES
If you find yourself without baking powder no problem. To ensure maximum crispiness coat chicken with cornstarch, all-purpose flour, rice flour or potato starch.
If you or friends and family like spicy food add red pepper flakes, a dash of hot sauce or a pinch of cayenne pepper to sauce mixture.
Low sodium soy sauce or reduced sodium tamari are great choices if you are watching your sodium intake. And tamari is also a gluten free option.

Air Fryer Whole Chicken

Servings: 5
Cooking Time: 1 Hour

Ingredients:

- 3 to 5 lb chicken innards removed
- 2 tbsp olive oil I use olive oil spray
- 2 tsp kosher salt
- 1 tsp freshly ground black pepper
- 1 tsp garlic powder
- 1 tsp paprika

Directions:

1. Combine the olive oil and spices and make a paste and rub it all over the chicken.
2. Give the air fryer basket a light spray of oil.
3. Place the chicken breast side down and cook at 350F for 30 minutes and then flip and cook breast side up for another 30 minutes.
4. Using a cooking thermometer check the thickest part of the breast to make sure the chicken has reached 165 F. Let rest for 5 to 10 minutes before serving.

Notes

Be sure to remove innards from the cavity before cooking if they didn't come removed. The giblets are great for making broth or gravy, so freeze them for the next time you make those!

Feel free to tie the legs together with twine and tuck the wings underneath if you're worried about it being overcooked. Some believe that tying the legs together will yield a juicier chicken, but I found it didn't make much of a difference.

Cooking time will vary depending on your air fryer and the size of your chicken. I use a Cosori 5.8 QT air fryer. I recommend you check in on your chicken at the 50-minute mark.

Make sure to pat the chicken dry before adding the seasoning paste to help it stick on better. It will also help the chicken crisp up as moisture will cause steam.

Let air fryer roasted chicken rest, so the juices redistribute. If you cut too early, the juices will end up on your cutting board.

If you have extra time and ingredients, stuff the inside of the chicken with fresh herbs such as rosemary and thyme, lemon wedges, and garlic cloves for additional flavor.

Air Fryer Trader Joe's Frozen Mandarin Orange Chicken

Servings: 5
Cooking Time: 12 Minutes

Ingredients:

- 22 ounces (624 g) Trader Joe's Frozen Mandarin Orange Chicken
- optional - chopped cilantro &/or green onion , for garnish
- optional - cooked rice to serve with chicken
- EQUIPMENT
- Air Fryer

Directions:

1. Place the frozen orange chicken in the air fryer basket and spread out into a single even layer. No oil spray is needed. Set the sauce aside (do not sauce the chicken yet).
2. Air Fry at 400°F/205°C for 8 minutes. Shake and flip the chicken pieces over and then continue to Air Fry at 400°F/205°C for another 2-4 minutes or until heated through and crispy.
3. Warm the orange sauce in microwave for 1 minute or on stovetop for 2-3 minutes on medium heat. Toss cooked chicken with as much sauce as desired. Garnish with optional cilantro and/or green onion and serve on cooked rice if desired.

Air Fryer Chicken Thighs

Servings: 4
Cooking Time: 18 Minutes

Ingredients:

- 4 bone-in chicken thighs
- 2 teaspoons paprika
- 1 teaspoons Italian Seasoning
- 1 teaspoon brown sugar
- 1/2 teaspoon salt
- 1/2 teaspoon pepper
- 2 Tablespoons olive oil

Directions:

1. Pat the chicken thighs with a paper towel to dry. Add them to a medium sized bowl.
2. In a small bowl combine paprika, Italian seasoning, brown sugar, and salt and pepper. Add the olive oil to the bowl of chicken and sprinkle with the seasonings and toss until fully coated.
3. Place the chicken thighs skin side down in the basket of the air fryer. Cook at 380 degrees for 10 minutes. Flip after 10 minutes and continue to cook for 7-8 more minutes until no longer pink and the internal temperature is 165 degrees.

Instant Pot & Vortex Roast Chicken

Servings: 4
Cooking Time: 33 Minutes

Ingredients:
- 1 chicken
- 1 Tbsp olive oil
- 2 Tbsp chicken spice
- 1 lemon
- Thyme
- 3 cloves garlic

Directions:
1. Rub the chicken with olive oil, salt, pepper & chicken spice.
2. Set the Instant Pot to Sauté and brown the chicken all around.
3. Remove from the pot.
4. Place the trivet into the Instant Pot.
5. Pour the white wine & stock into the base of the pot.
6. Cut the lemon in half and place in the cavity of the chicken with the garlic and fresh thyme.
7. Close the lid and set to High Pressure for 18 mins.
8. Allow a Natural Pressure Release.
9. Use the Saute function to thicken the sauce to make the gravy.
10. Serve with crushed potatoes or salad.

Air Fryer Kabobs

Servings: 4
Cooking Time: 12 Minutes

Ingredients:
- 1 pound chicken breast cut into 2 inch pieces
- 1 medium green bell pepper cut into 2 inch pieces
- 1 medium red bell pepper cut into 2 inch pieces
- 1 medium yellow bell pepper cut into 2 inch pieces
- 1 medium red onion cut into 2 inch pieces
- 1/2 tsp salt
- 1/4 tsp ground pepper
- 1 tbsp BBQ Sauce
- For Steak Kabobs
- 1 pound steak cut into 2 inch pieces

Directions:
1. If you are using chicken, pat cut it into pieces about two inches in size. For steak, cut it the same way, just skip rinsing it. Set the meat aside.
2. Cut the bell peppers and onion into two inch pieces.
3. To assemble the kabobs, just thread them on the skewer in any order or pattern you like.
4. Place the skewers in the air fryer basket, or in the tray and brush a light coating of BBQ sauce onto each piece, then season to taste with salt and pepper.
5. For steak, I cook the kabobs at 400 degrees F for 6 minutes on each side. For the chicken, I cook them at 380 degrees F for 5 minutes on each side.

Chicken Parmesan In The Air Fryer

Servings: 4
Cooking Time: 10 Minutes

Ingredients:
- 2 8 ounce boneless skinless chicken breasts (sliced lengthwise to make 4 thinner cutlets)
- 6 tbsp seasoned breadcrumbs (whole wheat or gluten-free)

- 2 tbsp grated Parmesan cheese
- 1 tbsp butter (melted (or olive oil))
- 6 tbsp reduced fat mozzarella cheese (I used Polly-o)
- 1/2 cup marinara
- olive oil spray

Directions:

1. Combine breadcrumbs and parmesan cheese in a bowl. Melt the butter in another bowl.
2. Lightly brush the butter onto the chicken, then dip into breadcrumb mixture.
3. When the air fryer is ready, transfer to the air fryer basket, in batches as needed and spray the top with oil.
4. Air fryer 360F° 5 minutes, turn and top each with 2 tbsp sauce and 1 1/2 tbsp of shredded mozzarella cheese.
5. Cook 3 more minutes or until cheese is melted.

Honey Bbq Wings

Servings: 4
Cooking Time: 25 Minutes

Ingredients:
- 2 pounds chicken wings
- 1 tablespoon olive oil
- salt and pepper to taste
- ¼ cup honey
- ¼ cup bbq sauce

Directions:
1. In the Air Fryer
2. Preheat the air fryer to 400°F.
3. Toss wings with olive oil, salt, and pepper. And place in the air fryer basket in a single layer. Cook for 15 minutes.
4. While wings are cooking, mix honey & bbq sauce in a small bowl.
5. After 15 minutes, remove the wings from the air fryer and toss them with the sauce.
6. I recommend lining the air fryer basket with parchment paper when adding the sauced wings Place the wings back in the air fryer basket and cook for an additional 5-7 minutes.

7. Let rest a few minutes before serving (the sauce will be very hot right after cooking).
Notes
For Oven Baked Wings
Toss the wings with 1 tablespoon flour, 1 teaspoon of baking powder and seasonings. Refrigerate 30 minutes (or up to 4 hours) uncovered.
Toss the wings with olive oil and place on rack that has been sprayed with cooking spray. Cook in a 425°F oven for 20 minutes, flip and bake an additional 15 minutes.
Toss with sauce and broil for a few minutes to crisp.
Optional additions to the bbq sauce: garlic, sriracha, fresh ginger, or hot pepper flakes
If using an air fryer, cook in a single layer and do not overcrowd the air fryer.
The sauce can be very sticky and difficult to clean from a baking pan or the air fryer basket. Line the baking pan or air fryer with parchment paper after adding the sauce to the wings.
Do not let the air fryer preheat or run with parchment without adding the wings to the fryer. The parchment can blow around and burn (the wings will hold it in place).
Cook in batches if needed. All batches can be reheated in the air fryer at 400°F for 2-3 minutes before serving.

Air Fryer Asian-glazed Boneless Chicken Thighs

Servings: 4
Cooking Time: 30 Minutes

Ingredients:
- 8 boneless, skinless chicken thighs, fat trimmed (32 oz total)
- 1/4 cup low sodium soy sauce
- 2 1/2 tablespoons balsamic vinegar
- 1 tablespoon honey
- 3 cloves garlic (crushed)
- 1 teaspoon Sriracha hot sauce
- 1 teaspoon fresh grated ginger
- 1 scallion (green only sliced for garnish)

Directions:

1. In a small bowl combine the balsamic, soy sauce, honey, garlic, sriracha and ginger and mix well.
2. Pour half of the marinade (1/4 cup) into a large bowl with the chicken, covering all the meat and marinate at least 2 hours, or as long as overnight.
3. Reserve the remaining sauce for later.
4. Preheat the air fryer to 400F.
5. Remove the chicken from the marinade and transfer to the air fryer basket.
6. Cook in batches 14 minutes, turning halfway until cooked through in the center.
7. Meanwhile, place the remaining sauce in a small pot and cook over medium-low heat until it reduces slightly and thickens, about 1 to 2 minutes.
8. To serve, drizzle the sauce over the chicken and top with scallions.

Air Fryer Whole Chicken Recipe
Servings: 4
Cooking Time: 55 Minutes

Ingredients:
- CHICKEN:
- 1 4-lb Whole chicken
- GARLIC BUTTER:
- 6 tbsp Danish Creamery European Style Unsalted Butter (softened)
- 3 cloves Garlic (crushed)
- 1 tbsp Fresh parsley
- 1 tbsp Fresh dill
- 1/4 tsp Sea salt
- SEASONING:
- 2 tbsp Olive oil
- 1/2 tsp Sea salt
- 1 tsp Paprika
- 1/2 tsp Black pepper

Directions:
1. In a small bowl, mash the butter with a fork. Add the garlic, parsley, dill, and sea salt. Mash again. Set aside.
2. Run your hands under the chicken skin on the breast and legs to separate it from the chicken underneath. Place dollops of garlic butter all over underneath the skin and then press down over the skin to spread around underneath.
3. Drizzle olive oil over the chicken, over the skin, on both sides. Sprinkle with sea salt, paprika, and black pepper, also on both sides.
4. Place the chicken in the air fryer basket, breast side down. Cook for 30 minutes at 350 degrees F (176 degrees C).
5. Flip the chicken over and cook for 25-35 more minutes, until a thermometer inserted in the thickest part of the breast reaches 160 degrees F (71 degrees C). Temperature will rise about 5 degrees while resting.
6. Remove chicken from the air fryer and let it rest for 10-15 minutes before carving.

Air Fryer Cornish Hen
Servings: 2-4
Cooking Time: 45 Minutes

Ingredients:
- 2 cornish hens, about 1.5 pounds each
- 2 tablespoons olive oil
- 2 teaspoon salt
- 1 1/2 teaspoons italian seasoning
- 1 teaspoon garlic powder
- 1 teaspoon paprika
- 1/2 teaspoon black pepper
- 1/2 teaspoon lemon zest (or 1 tablespoon lemon juice)

Directions:
1. Preheat your air fryer to 360 degrees.
2. In a small bowl, combine the oil and salt, Italian seasoning, garlic powder, paprika, black pepper, and lemon zest/juice.
3. Pat the cornish game hens dry with a paper towel then brush them with the seasoning mixture under and on top of the skin. Twist wings to tuck under the bird.
4. Place hen(s) in the air fryer basket, breast side down, and cook for 35 minutes.
5. Flip the hens and cook for an additional 10 minutes to get the skin crispy. Check internal temperature: hens are done at 165 degrees F. Serve and enjoy!
NOTES
HOW TO REHEAT CORNISH HEN IN THE AIR FRYER

Preheat your air fryer to 360 degrees.
Place the leftover Cornish hens in the air fryer and cook for about 18 minutes, until heated through. If reheating a half Cornish hen, reheat for just 3 to 4 minutes
Remove from the air fryer and enjoy!
HOW TO COOK FROZEN CORNISH HEN IN THE AIR FRYER
Preheat your air fryer to 360 degrees.
Place the hens in a single layer, spritz with cooking oil, and cook for 40 minutes until heated through. Flip the hens halfway through cooking.
Remove them from the air fryer and enjoy!

Cherry Glazed Chicken Wings

Ingredients:
- 12 chicken wings
- 3 tbsp canola oil, divided
- 1 garlic clove, minced
- 1 cup ketchup
- ½ cup apple cider vinegar
- ½ cup cherry preserves
- 2 tbsp Louisiana-style hot sauce
- 1 tbsp Worcestershire sauce
- 3 tsp salt, divided
- 1 tsp ground pepper, divided

Directions:
1. In a small saucepan, heat 1 tablespoon of oil over medium heat. Then, add in the garlic and cook and stir for 1 minute. Stir in ketchup, vinegar, cherry preserves, hot sauce, Worcestershire sauce, 1 teaspoon salt and ½ teaspoon pepper. Cook and stir until heated through.
2. Brush the wings with remaining oil and sprinkle with remaining salt and pepper.

3. Place the wings on the standard rack in the air fryer and air fry them at 350°F for 20 minutes, flipping halfway through. Brush with glaze during the last 5 minutes of air frying.
4. Serve with remaining glaze.

Air-fryer Chicken Wings
Servings: 2
Cooking Time: 35 Minutes

Ingredients:
- 2 teaspoons garlic powder
- 1 teaspoon garlic salt
- 1 teaspoon each ground mustard, ginger and nutmeg
- 1/2 teaspoon pepper
- 1/2 teaspoon ground allspice
- 1/2 teaspoon baking soda
- 1/2 teaspoon cayenne pepper
- 12 whole chicken wings (2-1/2 pounds)
- Optional: Ranch salad dressing, Buffalo sauce or barbecue sauce

Directions:
1. Preheat air fryer to 300°. In a large bowl, combine garlic powder, garlic salt, mustard, ginger, nutmeg, pepper, allspice, baking soda and cayenne.
2. Cut chicken wings into 3 sections; discard wing tip sections. Add to bowl with spices and stir to coat. In batches, arrange wings in a single layer on greased tray in air-fryer basket. Cook 15 minutes. Increase temperature to 400°; cook until chicken juices run clear and wings are golden brown, 20-25 minutes. Repeat with remaining wings. Serve hot, with dressing or sauce if desired.

BEEF, PORK & LAMB RECIPES

Air Fryer Prime Rib

Servings: 5-6
Cooking Time: 1 Hour 15 Minutes

Ingredients:

- 6 pound Prime Rib
- 3 tablespoons olive oil
- 1 ½ teaspoon salt
- 1 ½ teaspoon black pepper
- 1 teaspoon smoked paprika
- 1 teaspoon garlic powder
- ¼ cup minced garlic (about 10 cloves)
- One sprig fresh rosemary, chopped (or 1/2 teaspoon dried rosemary)
- One sprig fresh thyme, chopped (or 1/2 teaspoon dried thyme)

Directions:

1. Preheat your air fryer to 390 degrees.
2. Rub the prime rib with olive oil generously, then sprinkle it with salt, black pepper, paprika, and garlic powder.
3. Cover the prime rib with crushed garlic then the rosemary and thyme. I recommend using fresh rosemary and thyme for the best flavoring, but you can use dried as well.
4. Gently place the prime rib in the air fryer and cook for 20 minutes.
5. Leaving the prime rib steak in the air fryer, turn the temperature down
6. to 315 degrees and continue to cook for about 55 additional minutes until Instant-Read Thermometer reaches desired doneness -- 130 degrees for medium-rare.*
7. Let the prime rib sit for 20 to 30 minutes, then slice and enjoy!
NOTES
*if your thermometer is still reading too low, let prime rib cook in the air fryer for another 5 to 10 minutes, then check the temperature again
HOW TO REHEAT PRIME RIB IN THE AIR FRYER:
TO REHEAT FULL PRIME PRIME RIB:
Preheat your air fryer to 270 degrees.

Lay the prime rib in the air fryer and cook for about 10 to 15 minutes until warmed.
TO REHEAT PRE-COOKED PRIME RIB SLICES:
Preheat your air fryer to 400 degrees.
Place the prime rib slices in the air fryer in a single layer and cook for about 2 minutes. Use a parchment paper or silicone liner if the prime rib is sauced.

Air Fryer Sausage Patties

Servings: 6
Cooking Time: 10 Minutes

Ingredients:

- 1 pound ground pork
- 1 teaspoon salt
- ½ teaspoon black pepper
- ½ teaspoon fennel seeds slightly crushed
- ½ teaspoon garlic powder
- ½ teaspoon sage
- ½ teaspoon onion powder
- ⅛ teaspoon thyme leaves
- ⅛ teaspoon cayenne pepper

Directions:

1. Mix pork and seasonings in a medium bowl until fully combined. Refrigerate for at least 2 hours or overnight.
2. Preheat air fryer to 400°F.
3. Divide meat into 6 patties about ½ inch thick. Place in a single layer in the air fryer basket.
4. Cook for 5 minutes, flip the patties and cook them for another 4-5 minutes or until they reach 160°F internally.

Frozen Bacon In The Air Fryer

Servings: 3-4
Cooking Time: 22 Minutes

Ingredients:
- 1 pack of frozen bacon, regular sliced

Directions:
1. Wedge your block of bacon into your air fryer. It will be fine as long as you push it down far enough that you can properly close the air fryer.
2. Set your temperature on your air fryer to 360 degrees. The smoke point is 374 degrees, so I wanted to stay away from that. Cook it for 8 minutes. This gives your bacon time to defrost.
3. Once your bacon has softened, you will be able to use your tongs to pull the strips apart. I tried to separate and lay them as close to a single layer as possible, but overlap will happen since there is so much in there at once. As they cook down, the overlap will lessen.
4. Cook for an additional 10-14 minutes, checking frequently. To start, I would flip them with tongs every 3-4 minutes. Then at the 10 minute mark, I would remove strips that were the desired crispiness. Then I would space the remaining strips out more and check and flip every 2 minutes till they were all done.
5. Transfer them onto a paper towel lined plate to remove any excess grease. Serve and enjoy!

Tangy Smashed Brussels Sprouts With Bacon

Servings: 2
Cooking Time: 10 Minutes

Ingredients:
- ½ pound Brussels sprouts, halved
- 2 tablespoons orange marmalade
- 1 tablespoon Dijon mustard
- 1 tablespoon brown sugar
- 1 teaspoon apple cider vinegar
- 2 teaspoons kosher salt, divided
- 2 strips bacon, cut into ¼-inch pieces
- 1 tablespoon olive oil
- 1 teaspoon freshly ground black pepper
- 3 ounces Pecorino Romano, grated, for topping

Directions:
1. Bring a large pot of water to a boil over high heat.
2. Place the halved Brussels sprouts into the boiling water and cook for 6 to 7 minutes, then drain over a colander and pat dry with paper towels.
3. Place the orange marmalade, mustard, brown sugar, apple cider vinegar, and 1 teaspoon kosher salt in a large bowl and whisk until smooth.
4. Press each Brussels sprout half underneath the flat side of a knife or a bench scraper so that the sprout is flattened slightly. Place the smashed sprouts into a bowl.
5. Toss the sprouts with half of the orange marmalade sauce, bacon, olive oil, remaining kosher salt, and the pepper.
6. Place the crisper plate into the Smart Air Fryer basket.
7. Select the Preheat function, then press Start/Pause.
8. Place the Brussels sprouts onto the preheated crisper plate.
9. Select the Veggies function, adjust temperature to 415°F and time to 10 minutes, then press Start/Pause.
10. Shake the Brussels sprouts halfway through cooking. The Shake Reminder will let you know when.
11. Remove the Brussels sprouts when done and toss with the remaining orange marmalade sauce, then serve topped with the grated Pecorino Romano.

Air Fryer Bbq Ribs

Servings: 4
Cooking Time: 40 Minutes

Ingredients:
- 1 rack baby back ribs
- 2 tsp black pepper
- 1 tsp onion powder
- 1 tbsp brown sugar
- 1/4 tsp cayenne pepper optional for spice
- 1 cup BBQ sauce

Directions:

1. Preheat the air fryer to 380 degrees Fahrenheit.
2. Remove the membrane from the back of the ribs and then cut the rack in half to fit into the or Fryer basket.
3. Add all of the sugar and spice mixture into a small bowl and mix well.
4. Make sure the ribs dry, (you can use a paper towel for this) and rub the ribs on both sides with the seasoning.
5. Place the ribs into the preheated Air Fryer basket and cook for 18 minutes. Flip the ribs and cook for an additional 12 minutes.
6. Brush on the BBQ sauce (I prefer Sweet Baby Rays but you can use your favorite or even a homemade sauce!)
7. Increase the Air Fryer temperature to 400 degrees and cook for an additional 2-3 minutes.
8. Use a meat thermometer and make sure the ribs are cooked to the internal temperature of 145 degrees Fahrenheit. Carefully remove the ribs from the basket and allow them to rest under foil for 3-5 more minutes.
9. Add additional Bbq sauce and then slice as desired and serve.

NOTES

When cooking ribs, you should use a meat thermometer and ensure that the ribs have reached 145 degrees Fahrenheit.

Cooking times can vary depending on the size of the rack of ribs. I cook my ribs on average of 30-35 minutes from start to finish.

Once the ribs are all but fully cooked, add the barbecue sauce to the ribs and cook for an additional few minutes. After resting the ribs, add extra barbecue sauce if desired.

I prefer to use Sweet Baby Ray's barbecue sauce, but you can also use your favorite Bbq sauce or even a homemade BBQ sauce. You can make a homemade barbecue sauce quickly with a few bbq sauce ingredients such as ketchup, Worcestershire sauce, paprika, dry mustard, and red wine vinegar.

But if you're like me and want easy, just use your favorite store brand.

You can make your own homemade bbq spice rub with items such as onion powder, garlic powder, cayenne pepper, brown sugar, dry mustard, ground black pepper, and more. The sky is the limit for flavor and spices and it's all up to you and your preferred taste.

Air Fryer Breaded Pork Chops

Servings: 3
Cooking Time: 16 Minutes

Ingredients:

- 3 (6oz.) (3 (170g)) pork chops , rinsed & patted dry
- salt , to taste
- black pepper , to taste
- garlic powder , to taste
- smoked paprika , to taste
- 1/2 cup (54 g) breadcrumbs , approximately
- 1 large (1 large) egg
- Cooking spray , for coating the pork chops

Directions:

1. Add seasonings to both sides of the pork chops with salt, pepper, garlic powder, and smoked paprika.
2. Add the breadcrumbs in a medium bowl. In another bowl, beat the egg.
3. Dip each pork chop in egg and then dredge it in the breadcrumbs, coating completely. Lightly spray both sides of coated pork chops with cooking spray right before cooking.
4. Preheat the Air Fryer at 380°F for 4 minutes. This will give the pork chops a nice crunchy crust.
5. Place in the Air Fryer and cook at 380°F (194°C) for 8-12 minutes. After 6 minutes of cooking, flip the pork chops and then continue cooking for the remainder of time or until golden and internal temperature reaches 145-160°F.
6. Serve warm.

NOTES

Recipes were cooked in 3-4 qt air fryers. If using a larger air fryer, the recipe might cook quicker so adjust cooking time.

If cooking in multiple batches & not pre-heating before first batch, the first batch will take longer to cook.

Preheating the Air Fryer is preferable. If you don't preheat, add more time to the cooking.

Remember to set a timer to shake/flip/toss the food as directed in recipe.

Bbq Air Fryer Ribs

Servings: 4
Cooking Time: 35 Minutes

Ingredients:
- 1 3 lb rack of pork baby back ribs cut in half, membrane removed
- 3 Tablespoon bbq rub
- ?-1 cup bbq sauce

Directions:
1. Season the ribs with bbq spice rub, covering both sides of the ribs.
2. Preheat the air fryer to 380 degrees Fahrenheit for a few minutes, then place the ribs in the air fryer basket, meat side down and cook for 20 minutes.
3. Once the 20 minutes is up, grab a pair of tongs and flip the ribs over, and cook for an additional 10 minutes on 380 degrees.
4. Once the timer is up, open the basket and cover with the bbq sauce. Return to Air fryer and cook for 5 minutes on 400 degrees Fahrenheit.
5. Remove and allow the ribs to rest for a few minutes. Feel free to cover with additional bbq sauce if you like saucy ribs.

Notes

The cook times in this recipe are for pork baby back ribs. Beef ribs will likely take longer to cook.

I used my large air fryer (5.3qt) to ensure all my ribs would fit into the basket.

Air Fryer Meatloaf

Servings: 4
Cooking Time: 16 Minutes

Ingredients:
- 1 1/2 pounds ground beef
- 1 cup bread crumbs
- 1 large egg
- 2/3 cup milk
- 1/2 medium onion chopped
- 1 garlic clove minced
- 1 teaspoon salt
- 1/2 teaspoon pepper
- Meatloaf Sauce
- 1/2 cup ketchup
- 2 tablespoons brown sugar
- 1 teaspoon mustard
- 1 teaspoon Worcestershire Sauce

Directions:
1. In a large mixing bowl, combine the ground beef, bread crumbs, egg, milk, onion, and seasonings. Stir together until the ingredients are well mixed and onion and seasonings are evenly distributed throughout the ground beef.
2. Shape the meatloaf into a loaf and place on top of a piece of air fryer parchment paper or small pan or tray. Air fry at 380 degrees F for 16-18 minutes.
3. While the meatloaf is cooking, in a small bowl, combine the ketchup, brown sugar, mustard and Worcestershire Sauce. Stir together until well combined.
4. Once the meatloaf is done cooking, open basket, and brush sauce on top. Return basket to air fryer and air fry at 380 degrees F for an additional 2-3 minutes.

NOTES

For additional flavor, you can also add ¼ cup of bell pepper to your meatloaf.

Because air fryers are different, cooking time may need to be adjusted based on wattages and type of air fryer.

Air Fryer Lamb Chops

Servings: 8

Ingredients:
- 8 small lamb chops bone-in
- 1/2 teaspoon salt
- 1/4 teaspoon pepper
- 2 tablespoons olive oil
- 1 tablespoon butter
- 3 cloves garlic minced
- 2 tablespoons parsley chopped

Directions:
1. Preheat the air fryer to 190C/370F. Grease the air fryer basket.
2. Pat dry each lamb chop and cut off excess fat or sinew.
3. Add the chops to a large mixing bowl. In a small bowl, whisk together the olive oil, butter, garlic, and fresh rosemary. Toss through the chops, ensuring each one is well coated in the mix.
4. Add the chops in a single layer in the basket. Air fryer for 7-8 minutes, flip, and cook for another 7-8 minutes.
5. Let the meat rest for two minutes before serving.
Notes
TO STORE: Place them in an airtight container and store them in the refrigerator for up to four days.
TO FREEZE: Place the cooked and cooled chops in a ziplock bag and store them in the freezer for up to two months.
TO REHEAT: Reheat in the air fryer, oven or skillet.

Meatball Sliders

Servings: 9
Cooking Time: 19 Minutes

Ingredients:
- Sliders:
- 3 tablespoons unsalted butter
- 4 cloves garlic, minced
- 9 store-bought pull-apart dinner rolls
- 1 cup prepared tomato sauce
- ½ cup shredded Italian cheese blend
- 2 tablespoons fresh basil, chopped

- Meatballs:
- 2 tablespoons olive oil
- 1 small onion, finely diced
- 3 cloves garlic, minced
- ½ teaspoon red pepper flakes
- 1 pound grass-fed ground beef
- 2 tablespoons fresh parsley, finely chopped
- 1 large egg
- ¼ cup plain breadcrumbs
- 1/4 cup Parmesan cheese, freshly grated
- 1½ teaspoons kosher salt
- 1 teaspoon black pepper
- Olive oil spray

Directions:
1. Place olive oil in a small skillet over medium heat to start the meatballs.
2. Add the diced onion and sauté until translucent and lightly golden, about 3 minutes.
3. Add the minced garlic and red pepper flakes and sauté for another minute.
4. Remove the skillet from the heat and let cool to room temperature.
5. Transfer the cooled onions and garlic to a large bowl.
6. Add the beef, parsley, egg, breadcrumbs, Parmesan cheese, salt, and pepper, and mix with your hands until well combined.
7. Shape all of the mixture into 2-inch balls.
8. Select the Preheat function on the Smart Air Fryer, then press Start/Pause.
9. Place the meatballs into the preheated air fryer and lightly spray the tops with oil spray.
10. Set temperature to 400°F and time to 12 minutes, then press Start/Pause.
11. Remove the meatballs when done and transfer to a plate.
12. Note: Clean the air fryer basket before continuing.Place butter in a small skillet over medium heat to start the sliders.
13. Add the minced garlic once the butter is sizzling, then turn off the heat. Let the garlic infuse the butter for 5 minutes.
14. Cut a 2-inch-diameter circle into the top of each roll without cutting all the way through, creating a well. Discard the removed bread.

15. Brush the garlic butter over the outside and inside of each roll.
16. Line the air fryer basket with foil that goes up the sides of the basket.
17. Place the rolls into the air fryer basket.
18. Set temperature to 400°F and time to 5 minutes, then press Start/Pause.
19. Remove the rolls when golden brown and lightly toasted.
20. Place 1 tablespoon of tomato sauce into the bottom of each well, then place the meatballs on top.
21. Top each meatball with another tablespoon of tomato sauce and sprinkle cheese over the whole roll.
22. Set temperature to 400°F and time to 2 minutes, then press Start/Pause.
23. Remove the sliders when done and the cheese is melted and golden.
24. Serve the sliders warm, topped with fresh basil.

Air Fryer Gluten Free Pork Chops

Servings: 4
Cooking Time: 13 Minutes

Ingredients:
- 2.5 pounds pork chops bone in or boneless, about 3-4 chops
- 1 large egg
- 2 tablespoons water
- 3/4 cup almond flour
- 1/3 cup parmesan cheese grated
- 1/2 teaspoon garlic powder
- 1/2 teaspoon kosher salt
- 1/4 teaspoon ground black pepper

Directions:
1. Preheat Air Fryer to 390F for 5 minutes.
2. In a shallow medium bowl whisk together the egg and water.
3. In a shallow, separate bowl, to make the dry mixture, combine the flour, cheese, and seasonings.
4. Pat pork chops dry with a paper towel. Then, dredge the pork chop in the egg mixture, coating both sides.

5. Once coated with egg, dredge each piece of meat through the second bowl with flour and seasoning mix, coating both sides.
6. Spray the inside of the air fryer basket with non-stick cooking spray and place chops in basket in a single layer. (Depending on the size of your air fryer basket and pork chops you may need to cook them individually)
7. Air fry at 390F for 13-15 minutes flipping it halfway through air frying cooking process. If using thinner chops, adjust cook time by 1-2 minutes.
8. Remove from the basket when meat thermometer reads an internal temperature of at least 145F.
9. Let pork chops rest about 5 minutes before cutting. Season pork chops with your favorite seasonings.
NOTES
For a more intense flavor, you can add a sprinkle of chili powder, red pepper flakes, Italian seasonings, or cayenne pepper. For a mild flavor, leave those out, but add in a little more garlic powder.

Balsamic Glazed Pork Tenderloin Skewers

Ingredients:
- 1 lb. pork tenderloin, cubed
- 1 Tbsp. smoked paprika
- 1 tsp salt
- 1 tsp black pepper
- 1 tsp onion powder
- 1/2 tsp garlic powder
- 1/2 tsp white pepper
- 1/4 cayenne pepper
- 1/4 cup balsamic vinegar
- 2 tsp olive oil
- 1 Tbsp. Dijon mustard
- 3 Tbsp. honey
- 10 oz cherry tomatoes
- 1 red onion, largely chopped

Directions:
1. Trim and cube the pork tenderloin and set aside.

2. Make the dry rub for the pork by adding all of the seasonings to a bowl and mix.

3. Add the dry rub to the pork and mix well until all sides of the pork are coated.

4. Next mix the balsamic vinegar, olive oil, Dijon mustard and honey together to make the glaze. Set aside.

5. Spear the pork tenderloin, red onion and tomatoes onto the skewer and repeat. Attach each skewer to the Rotisserie Skewer accessory. See page 16 of the manual for more information on how to use this accessory.

6. Separate half the glaze into another small bowl and reserve for later. Brush the skewers with the glaze.

7. Insert the Rotisserie Skewer accessory into the oven and cook using the Kebab setting (370°F for 12 minutes).

8. Throughout the cooking process, glaze the skewers.

9. Once finished cooking, remove the Rotisserie Skewer accessory using the Rotisserie Tong.

10. Use the reserved glaze for and give the skewers one last glaze. Or, you can use this reserved glaze as a dipping sauce!

11. We sprinkled feta cheese and basil to these to finish them off!

Air Fryer Steak

Servings: 4
Cooking Time: 15 Minutes

Ingredients:
- 2 1-pound t-bone steaks
- 2 teaspoons olive oil
- 2 tablespoons Montreal steak seasoning, or your favorite steak rub

Directions:
1. Bring the steaks to room temperature for 15 minutes.

2. Rub the olive oil over the steak, then season with steak seasoning.

3. Preheat the air fryer to 400 degrees F. Place the steak in the air fryer basket. Air fry for 9-10 minutes for rare, 11-13 minutes for medium, 13-15 for medium-well.

4. Flip the steaks over halfway during the cooking process. Make sure you take the thickness of your steak into consideration when cooking — thicker steaks will take a bit longer.

5. Remove the steak and let it rest for 10 minutes before serving with your favorite sides.

NOTES
HOW TO COOK FROZEN STEAK IN THE AIR FRYER:
Prepare the steaks through step 2, then freeze them in a plastic zipper bag.

When ready to cook, spray the inside of the air fryer basket with non-stick spray. Place the frozen steak inside in a single layer.

Cook at 400 degrees F for 15 minutes, then flip and cook for 10-15 more minutes, to your desired doneness.

HOW TO REHEAT STEAK IN THE AIR FRYER:
Spray the inside of the air fryer basket, then place the steak inside.

Air fry at 400 degrees F for 8 minutes, until warmed through.

Air Fryer Italian Pork Chops Parmigiana

Servings: 3
Cooking Time: 18 Minutes

Ingredients:
- 3 (6 oz.) ((170g)) pork chops , rinsed & patted dry
- salt , to taste
- black pepper , to taste
- garlic powder , to taste
- smoked paprika , to taste
- 1/2 cup (54 g) breadcrumbs , approximately
- 1/2 cup (50 g) grated parmesan cheese
- 2 Tablespoons (30 ml) chopped Italian parsley , plus more for optional garnish
- 1 large egg
- Cooking spray , for coating the pork chops
- 1/2 cup (56 g) grated mozzarella cheese
- 1 cup (240 ml) marinara sauce , heated

Directions:
1. Season the pork chops with salt, pepper, garlic powder, and smoked paprika. In medium bowl, mix together the breadcrumbs, parmesan cheese, and chopped parsley. In another bowl, beat the egg.
2. Dip each pork chop in egg and then dredge it in the breadcrumb mixture, coating completely. Lightly spray both sides of coated pork chops with cooking spray right before cooking.
3. Preheat the Air Fryer at 380°F for 4 minutes.
4. Place in the Air Fryer and cook at 380°F (194°C) for 8-12 minutes.
5. After 6 minutes of cooking, flip the pork chops and then continue cooking for the remainder of time or until golden and internal temperature reaches 145-160°F. Top with cheese and air fry for 2 more minutes to melt the cheese. Serve warm with marinara sauce.
Notes
Recipes were cooked in 3-4 qt air fryers. If using a larger air fryer, the recipe might cook quicker so adjust cooking time.
If cooking in multiple batches & not pre-heating before first batch , the first batch will take longer to cook.
Remember to set a timer to shake/flip/toss the food as directed in recipe.
Preheating the Air Fryer is preferable. If you don't preheat, add more time to the cooking.

Air Fryer Flank Steak With Homemade Chimichurri Sauce
Servings: 4
Cooking Time: 20 Minutes

Ingredients:
- Steak:
- 2 pounds flank steak
- Chimichurri Sauce:
- 1/2 cup diced parsley
- 1/2 cup diced cilantro
- 1/2 onion
- 1 teaspoon kosher salt
- 1/2 teaspoon black pepper
- 1 teaspoon garlic

- 1/2 teaspoon red pepper flakes
- 1/3 cup olive oil
- 2 tablespoons red wine vinegar

Directions:
1. Let the flank steak get to room temperature, which will be about 15 to 30 minutes.
2. Preheat your air fryer to 400 degrees F, air fryer setting, for about 5 minutes.
3. Rub the olive oil or butter all over the steak, and season with salt and pepper.
4. Set the steaks in the air fryer for 15-20 minutes, flipping halfway.
5. Remove the steak, and let it rest for about 5 minutes before slicing.
6. Check the internal temperature of the steak, which should be 135 degrees F.
7. Plate, serve, and enjoy!

Dijon Steak Tips
Servings: 4
Cooking Time: 12 Minutes

Ingredients:
- 2 pounds flat iron or flank steak, cut into 1-inch cubes
- 1 yellow onion, thinly sliced
- 2 slices bacon, diced
- 3 tablespoons Worcestershire sauce
- 3 tablespoons Dijon mustard
- 2 tablespoons olive oil
- 2 tablespoon maple syrup
- 1 ½ teaspoon kosher salt
- 1 teaspoon paprika
- 2 tablespoons chopped fresh parsley, for garnish
- Mashed potatoes, for serving

Directions:
1. Select Preheat on the Air Fryer, adjust the temperature to 400°F, then press Start/Pause.
2. Stir together the steak, onion, bacon, Worcestershire, Dijon, oil, maple syrup, salt, and paprika in a medium bowl until evenly combined.
3. Place the meat mixture into the preheated air fryer.

4. Set the temperature to 400°F and time to 12 minutes, then press Start/Pause.
5. Shake the steak tips halfway through cooking.
6. Remove the steak when done, then serve garnished with parsley on a bed of mashed potatoes.

Air Fryer Pork Chops
Servings: 4
Cooking Time: 24 Minutes

Ingredients:
- 4 (3/4 to 1-inch thick) boneless center cut pork chops (about 6 ounces each), trimmed if needed
- 1 teaspoon kosher salt
- 1 large egg
- 1 tablespoon Dijon mustard
- 1/2 cup panko breadcrumbs
- 1/4 cup fine, dried breadcrumbs
- 1/4 cup finely grated Parmesan cheese
- 1/2 teaspoon garlic powder
- 1/2 teaspoon onion powder
- Cooking spray

Directions:
1. Set an air fryer to 400F and let heat for at least 10 minutes. Meanwhile, prepare the pork chops.
2. Season the pork chops all over with the salt and set aside. Whisk the egg and mustard together in a shallow dish. Shake the panko breadcrumbs, fine breadcrumbs, Parmesan, garlic powder, and onion powder together in a gallon zip-top bag.
3. Dip each pork chop in the egg mixture to coat, then place in the breadcrumb bag. When all 4 pork chops are in the bag, seal and shake to coat the chops evenly in the crumbs.
4. Coat the air fryer basket with cooking spray. Use tongs to transfer 2 pork chops into the air fryer and place in a single layer. Cook for 6 minutes. Flip and cook for 6 minutes more. The chops are done when the coating is golden brown and they register 145F in the thickest part with a probe thermometer. Repeat with the remaining 2 pork chops.
NOTES

Storage: Leftovers can be refrigerated in an airtight container for up to 4 days.

Air-fryer Sweet And Smoky Pork Tenderloin With Butternut Squash
Servings: 2
Cooking Time: 1 Hour

Ingredients:
- 1¼ pounds butternut squash, peeled, seeded, and cut into ¾-inch pieces (5 cups)
- 1 tablespoon
- unsalted butter,
- melted
- Salt and pepper
- 3½ teaspoons
- molasses
- 1 teaspoon smoked paprika
- 1 garlic clove, minced
- 1 (1-pound) pork tenderloin, trimmed and halved crosswise
- 1 teaspoon grated lime zest plus 1 teaspoon juice
- 2 tablespoons roasted pepitas
- 1 tablespoon minced fresh chives

Directions:
1. Toss squash with 1½ teaspoons melted butter, 1/8 teaspoon salt, and 1/8 teaspoon pepper in large bowl; transfer to air-fryer basket. Place basket in air fryer and set temperature to 350 degrees. Cook squash for 8 minutes, tossing halfway through cooking.
2. Meanwhile, microwave 3 teaspoons molasses, paprika, garlic, ½ teaspoon salt, and ½ teaspoon pepper in now-empty bowl until fragrant, about 30 seconds, stirring halfway through microwaving. Pat pork dry with paper towels, add to molasses mixture, and toss to coat.
3. Stir squash, then arrange tenderloin pieces on top. (Tuck thinner tail end of tenderloin under itself as needed to create uniform pieces.) Return basket to air fryer and cook until pork registers 140 degrees, 16 to 21 minutes, flipping and rotating tenderloin pieces halfway through cooking. Transfer pork

to large plate, tent with aluminum foil, and let rest while finishing squash.

4. Whisk lime zest and juice, remaining ½ teaspoon molasses, and remaining 1½ teaspoons melted butter together in medium bowl. Add squash, pepitas, and chives and toss to coat. Season with salt and pepper to taste. Slice pork ½ inch thick and serve with squash.

Air Fryer Ham And Cheese Croquettes

Servings: 20
Cooking Time: 35 Minutes

Ingredients:
- 1kg white potatoes, peeled, chopped
- 100g leg ham, chopped
- 80g (1 cup) coarsely grated cheddar
- 2 green shallots, chopped
- 50g (1/3 cup) plain flour
- 2 eggs
- 100g (2 cups) panko breadcrumbs
- Tonkatsu sauce, to serve
- Lemon wedges, to serve
- Select all Ingredients:

Directions:
1. Place the potatoes in a large saucepan. Cover with cold water. Bring to the boil over high heat. Boil for 10-12 minutes or until tender. Drain well. Return to pan over low heat. Mash until smooth and any water has evaporated. Remove from heat. Transfer to a bowl. Set aside to cool completely.

2. Add ham, cheese and shallot to potato. Season with salt. Mix until well combined. Roll 2 level tablespoonfuls of mixture into a ball. Repeat with remaining mixture.

3. Place the flour in a bowl. Whisk the eggs in a small bowl. Add the breadcrumbs to another bowl. Toss 1 ball in flour. Shake off excess then dip in egg and roll in breadcrumbs to coat. Place on a plate. Repeat with remaining balls. Place in the fridge for 15 minutes.

4. Preheat air fryer to 200°C. Cook the croquettes, in 2 batches, for 8-10 minutes or

until golden. Drizzle over tonkatsu sauce and serve with lemon wedges.

Pork Roulade

Servings: 4

Ingredients:
- 1kg pork
- 150g cooked chestnuts
- 50g dried cranberries
- 50g breadcrumbs
- 3 tbsp softened butter
- 2 rashes of smokey streaky bacon
- 1 tsp thyme
- 2 tbsp parsley
- 14 tsp nutmeg
- Salt and pepper to taste

Directions:
1. Add chestnuts, breadcrumbs, butter, bacon, herbs and seasonings to a small blender and blend until well incorporated. Then add cranberries.

2. Cut pork in half ensuring you leave about 2cm intact at the end. Spread pork out and lightly pound it, then generously season with salt and pepper. Spread stuffing on top of pork evenly.

3. Roll meat up and then secure with cooking twine or toothpicks.

4. Insert pot in unit and close lid. Select ROAST, then PRESET. Using the up and down arrows select PORK and set temperature to MED-WELL. Press START/STOP to begin preheating.

5. While unit is preheating, mix maple syrup, oil, paprika, salt and pepper in a small bowl or a cup. Pour small amount over meat and spread it evenly.

6. When unit beeps to signify it has preheated, insert probe to the middle of the side of the roast. Place meat in the unit, cover with tin foil and close lid to begin cooking.

7. After 45 minutes, open lid, remove tin foil and brush more marinade on top of meat. Close lid to continue.

8. When cooking is complete, carefully remove probe, set roast aside and allow to rest for 10 minutes.
9. Enjoy with side of vegetables.

Air-fryer Corn Ribs
Servings: 4
Cooking Time: 25 Minutes

Ingredients:
- 4 corn cobs, husks and silks removed
- 3 tsp Cajun seasoning
- 2 tsp extra virgin olive oil
- 1/2 cup sour cream
- 2 tsp sriracha sauce
- 50g Danish-style feta, crumbled
- 1/4 bunch coriander, leaves picked, roughly chopped

Directions:
1. Cut ends of cobs to ensure a flat base. Working with 1 cob at a time, microwave on high on a microwave-safe plate, covered with paper towel for 1 minute to soften slightly. Place cob upright, with the largest base down, on a board and cut cob in half lengthways with a large, sharp knife. Cut each half into two wedges.
2. Repeat with remaining cobs.
3. Place corn, seasoning and oil in a large bowl. Rub to coat.
4. Preheat an air-fryer to 200°C. Place half the corn in air-fryer basket and cook for 10 minutes, tossing corn halfway through, or until corn is cooked through. Repeat with remaining corn.
5. Place sour cream in a small bowl. Add sriracha sauce and swirl to combine.
6. Place corn on a serving plate and sprinkle with feta and coriander. Serve with spicy sour cream.

Air Fryer Pork Loin
Servings: 6
Cooking Time: 35 Minutes

Ingredients:
- 2 1/2 to 3 pounds pork loin roast
- 1 teaspoon dried Italian seasoning
- 1/2 teaspoon garlic powder
- 1/2 teaspoon onion powder
- 1/2 teaspoon kosher salt
- 1/2 teaspoon black pepper

Directions:
1. Preheat your air fryer to 370 degrees F.
2. Whisk the Italian seasoning, garlic powder, onion powder, salt, and pepper in a small bowl.
3. Trim away any excess fat from the outside of the pork loin then rub the pork all over with the seasoning mix.
4. Place the pork loin in the air fryer and cook for 35 to 40 minutes,* flipping once halfway through cooking until the roast reaches an internal temperature of 145 degrees F.
5. Remove the pork loin from the air fryer and transfer it to a cutting board. Allow it to rest at least 5 minutes before slicing then enjoy!
NOTES
*Cook pork loin 12 to 14 minutes per pound
HOW TO REHEAT PORK LOIN IN THE AIR FRYER:
Preheat your air fryer to 370 degrees.
Cook the leftover pork loin for about 3 minutes until warmed thoroughly.
Remove the pork loin from the air fryer and enjoy!
HOW TO COOK FROZEN PORK LOIN IN THE AIR FRYER:
Preheat your air fryer to 370 degrees.
Place the frozen pork loin in the air fryer and cook for about 60 minutes, flipping halfway through until the roast hits 145 degrees internally.
Remove the pork loin from the air fryer, let rest for at least 5 minutes before slicing, then enjoy!

Lightly Fried Lamb Chops

Ingredients:
- 3 lamb rib chops
- 1 tbsp minced garlic
- 1 tbsp fresh rosemary, chopped
- ½ tsp dried crushed red pepper

Directions:
1. In a small bowl, combine the garlic, rosemary, and crushed red pepper, then rub about ¼ tsp of the mixture over both sides of each lamb chop
2. Sprinkle the lamb chops with salt and cover and refrigerate for up to 4 hours
3. Place the lamb chops in a 200°C air fryer and cook for approximately 10 minutes, shaking the basket halfway through

Air-fryer Mini Chimichangas

Servings: 14
Cooking Time: 10 Minutes

Ingredients:
- 1 pound ground beef
- 1 medium onion, chopped
- 1 envelope taco seasoning
- 3/4 cup water
- 3 cups shredded Monterey Jack cheese
- 1 cup sour cream
- 1 can (4 ounces) chopped green chiles, drained
- 14 egg roll wrappers
- 1 large egg white, lightly beaten
- Cooking spray
- Salsa

Directions:
1. In a large skillet, cook beef and onion over medium heat until meat is no longer pink; crumble meat; drain. Stir in taco seasoning and water. Bring to a boil. Reduce heat; simmer, uncovered, for 5 minutes, stirring occasionally. Remove from the heat; cool slightly.

2. Preheat air fryer to 375F. In a large bowl, combine cheese, sour cream and chiles. Stir in beef mixture. Place an egg roll wrapper on work surface with a corner facing you. Place 1/3 cup filling in center. Fold bottom one-third of wrapper over filling; fold in sides.
3. Brush top point with egg white; roll up to seal. Repeat with remaining wrappers and filling. (Keep remaining egg roll wrappers covered with waxed paper to keep them from drying out.)
4. In batches, place chimichangas in a single layer on greased tray in air-fryer basket; spritz with cooking spray. Cook until golden brown, 3-4 minutes on each side. Serve warm with salsa and additional sour cream.

Air Fryer Bacon Wrapped Cream Cheese Crackers

Servings: 4
Cooking Time: 10 Minutes

Ingredients:
- 12 club crackers
- 4 ounces cream cheese softened
- 1 teaspoon onion powder
- 6 slices bacon halved

Directions:
1. Add the onion powder to the softened cream cheese and mix until combined.
2. Add a teaspoon of the cream cheese mixture to the top of the cracker.
3. Wrap the cracker in a slice of bacon. Continue wrapping the crackers until they are all finished.
4. Place the bacon wrapped crackers in a single layer in the basket of the air fryer.
5. Air fry the crackers at 350 degrees Fahrenheit for 7-9 minutes or until the bacon is brown and reached your desired level of crispiness.
6. Carefully remove from the air fryer and serve immediately.

FISH & SEAFOOD RECIPES

Air Fryer Shrimp

Servings: 4
Cooking Time: 4 Minutes

Ingredients:
- 1 lb. raw large shrimp, tail on and deveined
- 2 teaspoons kosher salt separated
- ½ teaspoon ground black pepper
- ½ teaspoon paprika
- 1 tablespoon fresh lemon juice
- ¾ cup panko crumbs
- ½ cup shredded parmesan cheese or pecorino romano
- 2 large eggs

Directions:
1. Rinse the shrimp under cold water and pat dry. Transfer the shrimp to a bowl. Add 1 teaspoon kosher salt, pepper, paprika, and lemon juice to the shrimp and toss until coated. Set aside for 15 minutes.
2. While the shrimp is marinating, mix the panko crumbs, cheese, and 1 teaspoon of salt in a bowl. Crack the eggs into a separate bowl and whisk.
3. After 15 minutes, preheat the air fryer to 400°F.
4. Dredge a shrimp through the egg wash and allow excess egg to drip from the shrimp. Place the shrimp on a plate and sprinkle with the panko mixture until evenly coated. Dredge the shrimp through the egg wash a second time and repeat the breading process. Set the shrimp on a plate. Repeat until all the shrimp are coated. We highly recommend breading the shrimp on a plate rather than directly in the bowl with the panko mixture so the mixture doesn't become soggy and unable to stick to the shrimp.
5. Drizzle olive oil in the bottom of the air fryer and transfer the shrimp to the air fryer. Be sure the shrimp are not touching the air fryer.
6. Air fry the shrimp for 2 minutes, flip the shrimp and fry for another 2 minutes. Remove the shrimp from the air fryer and repeat until all the shrimp are golden brown and cooked.
7. Serve the shrimp on their own with a fresh squeeze of lemon, with a marinara sauce, or on top of a salad.
8. Air fryer shrimp on a plate with sliced lemons.

Tips & Notes
We used large shrimp for this recipe. You can use medium shrimp or jumbo shrimp if you want to, but you may need more egg wash and panko mixture.
The process of breading the shrimp takes some time, so be patient.
You can substitute breadcrumbs for the panko crumbs if desired.

Chili-lime Air Fryer Salmon

Servings: 4
Cooking Time: 10 Minutes

Ingredients:
- 4 6 ounce pieces wild salmon fillet, skin on
- 1 1/4 teaspoons Tajin Classic or chili-lime seasoning
- 1/4 teaspoon kosher salt
- 1/2 teaspoon garlic powder
- 1/2 teaspoon oregano
- 1/4 teaspoon smoked paprika
- Lime wedges (for serving)
- chopped fresh cilantro
- mango-avocado salsa (Optional for topping)

Directions:
1. Spritz salmon all over with oil and season with chili-lime seasoning, garlic powder, paprika, oil, 1/4 teaspoon salt and oregano.
2. Spray the basket with olive oil or use air fryer parchment with holes to prevent sticking.
3. Place salmon in the air fryer basket with the skin side down and air fry 400F for 6 to 8 minutes.
4. Serve with lime wedges and top with fresh cilantro, and optional salsa if desired.

5. Oven Directions:
6. Bake on a sheetpan in a preheated 400F oven about 10 minutes.

Air Fryer Parmesan Shrimp

Ingredients:
- 2 pounds jumbo cooked shrimp, peeled and deveined
- 4 cloves garlic, minced
- 2/3 cup parmesan cheese, grated
- 1 teaspoon pepper
- 1/2 teaspoon oregano
- 1 teaspoon basil
- 1 teaspoon onion powder
- 2 tablespoons olive oil
- Lemon, quartered

Directions:
1. In a large bowl, combine garlic, parmesan cheese, pepper, oregano, basil, onion powder and olive oil.
2. Gently toss shrimp in mixture until evenly-coated.
3. Spray air fryer basket with non-stick spray and place shrimp in basket.
4. Cook at 350 degrees for 8-10 minutes or until seasoning on shrimp is browned.
5. Squeeze the lemon over the shrimp before serving.
Notes
If using an oven, bake at 400 degrees for 6-8 minutes.

Air Fryer Tilapia
Servings: 4
Cooking Time: 6 Minutes

Ingredients:
- 4 5-oz Tilapia fillets
- 2 tbsp Olive oil
- 2 tsp Lemon pepper seasoning (with salt; add 3/4 teaspoon sea salt if yours is unsalted)
- 1/2 tsp Paprika
- 1/4 tsp Garlic powder
- 1 medium Lemon (optional; sliced into wedges)
- Fresh parsley (optional, for garnish)

Directions:
1. Preheat the air fryer to 400 degrees F (204 degrees C). Lightly spray the basket with cooking spray.
2. In a small bowl, whisk together olive oil, lemon pepper seasoning, paprika, and garlic powder.
3. Brush both sides of each tilapia fillet with olive oil/spice mixture, until evenly coated.
4. Place tilapia in the air fryer basket in a single layer, so they are not touching each other. (Cook in batches if it doesn't all fit.) Cook for 6-8 minutes, until the tilapia is lightly browned and easily flakes with a fork.
5. Remove the fish from the air fryer. If desired, squeeze a lemon wedge onto each tilapia fillet and garnish with parsley before serving.

Air Fryer Salmon
Servings: 2
Cooking Time: 8 Minutes

Ingredients:
- 2 salmon fillets about 6 ounces each
- Pinch kosher salt
- Pinch black pepper
- 1 tablespoon brown sugar or honey
- 1 tablespoon Dijon mustard
- 1/2 tablespoon extra virgin olive oil
- 1/2 tablespoon low sodium soy sauce
- 1/4 teaspoon garlic powder
- Pinch ground ginger optional

Directions:
1. With paper towels, pat the salmon dry. Sprinkle lightly on both sides with salt and pepper.
2. For easy cleanup, line the air fryer basket with aluminum foil. Preheat the air fryer to 400 degrees F according to the manufacturer's instructions (for my air fryer, that is 3 minutes).
3. In a small bowl or larger liquid measuring cup, mix together the brown sugar, Dijon, oil, soy sauce, garlic powder, and ginger (if using). Spoon all over the top of the salmon.

4. Slide out the air fryer basket and set it on a heatproof surface. Place the fillets in the basket so that they are not touching.

5. Cook the salmon in the air fryer for 6 to 11 minutes, depending upon their thickness and your model (fillets around 1 inch will need 8 to 9 minutes). Do not overcook or the salmon will be dry. Salmon is done when it registers 145 degrees F on an instant read thermometer (I remove mine a few degrees early, let it rest, then the carryover cooking finishes the job). Check it a few times towards the end to make sure it doesn't overcook.

6. Transfer to a serving plate. Enjoy hot, with a sprinkle of additional salt and pepper as desired.

Notes

TO STORE: Refrigerate salmon in an airtight storage container for up to 2 days.

TO REHEAT: Gently reheat leftovers in a skillet on the stovetop over medium-low heat until just warmed through.

Air Fryer Haddock

Servings: 4
Cooking Time: 10 Minutes

Ingredients:
- 4 6 oz haddock filets, skinless
- 1 tablespoon olive oil
- 1 teaspoon Italian seasoning
- ½ teaspoon garlic powder
- ½ teaspoon paprika
- ½ teaspoon kosher salt
- ¼ teaspoon black pepper
- Lemon wedges, for serving
- SERVE WITH: greens, rice, pasta, fresh steamed vegetables

Directions:
1. Pat the fish dry with paper towels and place them on a cutting board.
2. Drizzle the fillets with oil, then sprinkle them on the fleshy sides liberally with the seasonings.
3. Place the filets in a single layer in the air fryer without overcrowding.

4. Air fry at 350 degrees F for 8-10 mins, until fully cooked and opaque. Serve as desired.

5. FROM FROZEN:
6. Prepare the fish through step 2, then store the filets in a plastic zipper bag and freeze.
7. When ready to cook, Preheat the air fryer to 350 degrees F for about 5 minutes.
8. Place the filets in a single layer in the air fryer, without overcrowding.
9. Air fry at 350 degrees F for 9-12 mins, until fully cooked and opaque. Serve as desired.

NOTES

HOW TO REHEAT HADDOCK:

Preheat the air fryer to 350 degrees.

Place haddock in air fryer and cook for 3-5 minutes or until hot.

Giant Air Fryer Potato Rosti

Servings: 2
Cooking Time: 35 Minutes

Ingredients:
- 750g washed desiree potatoes, peeled, coarsely grated
- 1/2 tsp sea salt
- Topping 1 – Smoked salmon and sour cream
- 200g smoked salmon
- 100g sour cream
- 1 tbsp finely chopped chives
- Topping 2 – Mexican
- 35g (1/3 cup) grated cheddar OR Mexican cheese blend
- 1/2 avocado, mashed
- 30g chargrilled red capsicum, finely diced
- 2 tbsp drained black beans
- 2 tbsp sour cream
- Grated manchego cheese, to serve (optional)
- Lime wedges, to serve
- Topping 3 – Egg, bacon 'n' cheese
- 50g haloumi, grated
- 50g mozzarella, grated
- 25g parmesan, grated
- 2 eggs
- 5-6 rashers streaky bacon, rind removed

- Topping 4 - French onion
- 1/2 tub French onion dip
- 1 green shallot, finely sliced
- Select all ingredients

Directions:
1. Combine potato and salt in a bowl. Spray an air fryer basket with oil. Spread with the grated potato, pressing to the edges. Air fry at 200C for 25-30 minutes. Cool in the basket for 5 minutes before inverting onto a serving plate.
2. To make topping 1, spread potato rosti base with sour cream and arrange smoked salmon on top. Finish with a scatter of chives.
3. To make topping 2, scatter the potato rosti base with cheese and place under a hot oven grill for 5 minutes or until melted. Top with a generous spoonful of mashed avo, capsicum, black beans and a dollop of sour cream. Finish with a sprinkle of manchego, if desired. Serve with fresh lime wedges.
4. To make topping 3, scatter the potato rosti base with the cheeses and place under a hot oven grill for 5 minutes or until melted. Pan-fry eggs and bacon and arrange on top.
5. To make topping 4, dollop the potato rosti base with the French onion dip and scatter with shallot.

Perfect Air Fryer Salmon
Servings: 2
Cooking Time: 7-9 Minutes

Ingredients:
- 1 teaspoon smoked paprika
- 1 teaspoon kosher salt
- 1/2 teaspoon freshly ground black pepper
- 2 (6 to 8-ounce) skin-on salmon fillets (about 1 1/2 inches thick)
- 2 teaspoons olive oil

Directions:
1. Heat an air fryer for 10 minutes at 390°F.
2. Place 1 teaspoon smoked paprika, 1 teaspoon kosher salt, and 1/2 teaspoon black pepper in a small bowl and stir to combine. Check 2 salmon fillets for pin bones and remove any missed bones with tweezers or pliers. Season the salmon on all sides with the spice mixture. Drizzle the salmon with 2 teaspoons olive oil and rub to evenly coat.
3. Place the salmon skin-side down in the air fryer and cook until golden-brown on top and the flesh flakes at the end when gently tested with a fork, 7 to 9 minutes.
RECIPE NOTES
Storage: Leftovers can be refrigerated in an airtight container up to 2 days.

Fish And Sweet Potato Chips
Servings: 2
Cooking Time: 15 Minutes

Ingredients:
- 400g sweet potato, peeled, cut into fries
- 1 tsp rice bran oil
- 2/3 cup panko breadcrumbs
- 1 tsp lemon rind
- 1 egg
- 360g white fish fillets, cut into portions
- 1/2 cup Tamar Valley Dairy Greek Style Yoghurt
- 2 tbsp finely chopped gherkins
- 1/2 eschalot, finely chopped
- 1 1/2 tbsp finely chopped chives
- 2 tsp finely chopped dill
- Select all ingredients

Directions:
1. Preheat Philips Airfryer to 180C.
2. Place sweet potato and oil in a medium bowl and toss to coat. Place in basket. Arrange separating grill on top of sweet potato.
3. Combine breadcrumbs and rind on a shallow plate. Season with salt and pepper. Whisk egg on another shallow plate. Dip fish into egg to cover, then press into breadcrumbs to coat. Lightly spray with oil and place on separating grill. Place basket in Airfryer. Cook for 12 minutes or until fries are golden and tender and fish is golden and the flesh flakes with a fork.
4. Meanwhile, combine yoghurt, gherkins, eschalot, chives and dill in a medium bowl. Season with salt and pepper. Serve fish with sweet potato fries and homemade tartare sauce.

Air Fryer Shrimp In 8 Minutes

Servings: 4
Cooking Time: 7 Minutes

Ingredients:

- 1 lb shrimp large or extra large
- 1 tablespoon olive oil
- 1/2 tablespoon lemon juice
- 1/2 teaspoon salt
- 1/2 teaspoon pepper
- 1/2 teaspoon garlic
- 1/2 teaspoon smoked paprika
- 1 teaspoon Italian seasonings

Directions:

1. Pat dry shrimp with a paper towel.
2. In a mixing bowl, whisk together the olive oil and lemon juice. Add the seasonings and mix well. Toss through the shrimp in the seasoning mix.
3. Cook the shrimp at 200C/400F for 7-8 minutes.
4. Serve immediately.

Notes

TO STORE: Air fryer shrimp can be stored in the refrigerator for up to 3 days in an air-tight container.

TO FREEZE: Place leftovers in a ziplock bag and store it in the freezer for up to 2 months.

TO REHEAT: Thaw and then put on the baking sheet or in the air fryer basket to reheat until crispy.

Teriyaki Salmon In The Air Fryer

Servings: 3-4
Cooking Time: 10 Minutes

Ingredients:

- ½ cup low sodium soy sauce
- ¼ cup light brown sugar
- 2 tablespoons apple cider vinegar
- 2 tablespoons rice vinegar
- 2 teaspoon garlic powder
- ½ teaspoon onion powder
- ½ teaspoon ground ginger
- 1 tablespoon water
- 1 tablespoon cornstarch
- 3 salmon filets

Directions:

1. To make homemade teriyaki sauce, combine soy sauce, brown sugar, vinegars, and seasonings in a bowl.
2. In a separate small bowl, whisk cornstarch and water until the cornstarch is completely dissolved.
3. Pour the soy sauce mixture and cornstarch mixture into a saucepan and heat over medium-low for 3 to 4 minutes, till it begins to thicken. Once it has reached your desired thickness, remove from heat and allow to cool for a few minutes.
4. Preheat your air fryer to 390 degrees F. During this time, season your filets with a little salt and pepper and then, using a basting brush, brush about 2 tablespoons of teriyaki sauce on each filet.
5. Once your air fryer is preheated, lay a parchment sheet down or brush your basket with olive oil. Place your salmon filets in the basket and cook for 10 minutes, or until the internal temperature reaches 145 degrees F. The glaze should be a little sticky and crispy, but the inside nice and juicy.

NOTES

HOW TO REHEAT TERIYAKI SALMON IN THE AIR FRYER

Preheat the air fryer to 350 degrees F.

Place the salmon in the basket on top of the parchment mat.

Cook for 3 to 5 minutes until warmed through.

Blackened Air Fryer Salmon With Cucumber-avocado Salsa

Servings: 4
Cooking Time: 14 Minutes

Ingredients:

- The salmon:
- 1 tablespoon sweet paprika
- 1/2 teaspoon cayenne pepper
- 1 teaspoon garlic powder
- 1 teaspoon dried oregano
- 1 teaspoon dried thyme
- 3/4 teaspoon kosher salt
- 1/8 teaspoon freshly ground black pepper
- Olive oil spray

- 4 (6 oz each) wild salmon fillets
- The salsa:
- 2 tablespoons chopped red onion
- 1 1/2 tablespoons fresh lemon juice
- 1 teaspoon extra virgin olive oil
- 1/4 + 1/8 teaspoon kosher salt
- Freshly ground black pepper
- 4 Persian (mini) cucumbers* diced
- 6 ounces Hass avocado (1 large) diced

Directions:
1. The salmon:
2. In a small bowl, combine the paprika, cayenne, garlic powder, oregano, thyme, salt and black pepper.
3. Spray both sides fo the fish with oil and rub all over. Coat the fish all over with the spices.
4. Preheat the air fryer to 400 degrees F.
5. Working in batches, arrange the salmon fillets skin side down in the air fryer basket.
6. Cook until the fish flakes easily with a fork, 5 to 7 minutes, depending on the thickness of the fish. (For a toaster oven-style air fryer, the temperature and timing remain the same.)
7. Serve topped with the salsa.
8. The salsa:
9. In a medium bowl, combine the red onion, lemon juice, olive oil, salt and pepper to taste. Let stand for 5 minutes, then add the cucumbers and avocado.
Notes
Recipe printed with permission from The Skinnytaste Air Fryer Cookbook by Gina Homolka
*If Persian cucumbers are not available, use English cucumbers (unpeeled) instead.
Weight Watchers Points: 3 (Freestyle SmartPoints)

Wild Alaskan Salmon Jerky Treats
Servings: 20
Cooking Time: 4 Hr

Ingredients:
- 1 pound wild Alaskan salmon, skin and pin bones removed

- Spices or herbs safe for dogs (basil, ginger, parsley, turmeric), optional

Directions:
1. Slice the salmon into ¼-inch-thick pieces.
2. Place the salmon evenly between the Food Dehydrator trays. Sprinkle with dried spices or herbs if using.
3. Set temperature to 145°F and time to 4 hours, then press Start/Stop.
4. Remove when done, cool to room temperature on the trays, then serve to your pet.

Blackened Fish With Key Lime Tartar
Servings: 4
Cooking Time: 10 Minutes

Ingredients:
- Blackened Fish
- 1 tablespoon paprika
- 1/2 teaspoon dried cayenne pepper
- 1 teaspoon garlic powder
- 1 teaspoon dried thyme
- 1 teaspoon dried oregano
- 1 teaspoon kosher salt
- 1/8 teaspoon black pepper
- olive oil spray
- 4 pieces fresh skinned white fish fillets (6 ounces each (mahi mahi, grouper, red snapper, tilapia))
- 3 cups cooked wild rice or brown rice
- lime wedges (for serving)

Directions:
1. Combine the ingredients for the tartar sauce and refrigerate until ready to serve.
2. In a small bowl, combine the paprika, cayenne, garlic powder, thyme, oregano, salt, black pepper and mix to blend.
3. Spritz the fish with oil on both sides and rub all over.
4. Coat the fish on both sides with the spice mix.
5. Air Fryer Directions:
6. Spray the air fryer basket with oil. Working in batches, place the fish in the basket in a single layer and cook 400F until

the fish flakes easily with a fork, about 5 to 7 minutes, turning halfway depending on the thickness of the fish.
7. Oven Directions:
8. Broil fish 6" from heating element high, 4-5 minutes, no need to turn
9. To serve:
10. Place 3/4 cup rice on each plate, 1 piece of fish, and divide sauce in 4 tiny bowls. Serve with lime wedges.

Garlic Butter Air Fryer Salmon
Servings: 4
Cooking Time: 10 Minutes

Ingredients:
* 500 g (1lb) salmon fillets
* ½ cup melted butter
* 3 garlic cloves crushed
* 1 tsp oregano
* pinch of chilli flakes
* 2 tsp lemon juice
* 2 tsp parsley
* salt and pepper

Directions:
1. Combine melted butter, crushed garlic, oregano, chilli flakes, fresh parsley and lemon juice in a bowl and mix. Season with salt and pepper.
2. Season the salmon with salt and pepper on both sides.
3. Place the salmon, flesh-side down on a piece of parchment paper, then brush over half of the garlic butter.
4. Place in the air fryer and allow to cook at 200°C/390°F for 5 minutes or until the skin is crisp.
5. Gently turn over the salmon, remove the parchment paper and brush with the remaining garlic butter.
6. Place back in the air fryer and cook for another 3-5 minutes or until the salmon is cooked to your preference.
7. Remove and serve with lemon.

Air Fryer Garlic Butter Shrimp
Servings: 4
Cooking Time: 8 Minutes

Ingredients:
* 1 pound large shrimp thawed, peeled and deveined
* 1 ½ tablespoon olive oil
* 2 teaspoons lemon juice
* ½ teaspoon parsley
* ¼ teaspoon salt
* ¼ teaspoon pepper
* 2 garlic cloves minced

Directions:
1. Preheat air fryer to 370°F.
2. In a medium bowl toss shrimp with oil and seasonings.
3. Place shrimp in a single layer in an air fryer basket.
4. Cook for 3-4 minutes or until shrimp are cooked through.
Notes
Shrimp should be cooked in a single layer in the basket. To cook in batches, cook shrimp as directed. At the end, add all shrimp to the basket for the last minute of cooking to heat through.

Air Fryer Tilapia In 7 Minutes
Servings: 4
Cooking Time: 7 Minutes

Ingredients:
* 4 tilapia fillets 4-6 ounces each
* 1/2 teaspoon salt
* 1/2 teaspoon pepper
* 1/2 teaspoon garlic
* For the lemon butter sauce
* 1/4 cup butter melted
* 3 cloves garlic minced
* 1 tablespoon lemon juice
* 1 tablespoon parsley

Directions:
1. Preheat the air fryer to 200C/400F. Spray the basket with cooking spray.
2. Pat dry the tilapia fillets. Mix the salt, pepper, smoked paprika, and garlic and using

your hands, rub the spices over both sides of the fish.

3. Add the tilapia filets in the air fryer basket and spray the top with cooking spray. Air fry for 7-8 minutes, flipping halfway through.

4. While the fish is cooking, make the sauce. In a small bowl, whisk together the melted butter, garlic, lemon juice and parsley.

5. Brush the lemon butter sauce generously over the top of the fish fillets and serve immediately.

Notes

TO STORE: Leftovers can be stored in the refrigerator, covered, for up to three days.

TO FREEZE: Place cooked and cooled tilapia can in an airtight container and stored in the freezer for up to two months.

TO REHEAT: Either microwave the fish for 20-30 seconds or reheat in the air fryer for 2 minutes, until crispy around the edges.

Crispy Popcorn Shrimp

Servings: 4
Cooking Time: 15 Minutes

Ingredients:

- 2 eggs
- 2 tablespoons water
- ½ cup all-purpose flour
- ½ teaspoon each salt & pepper
- 1 cup Panko bread crumbs
- ½ cup seasoned bread crumbs
- 2 teaspoons garlic powder
- 1 teaspoon smoked paprika
- 1 pound uncooked small shrimp peeled and deveined
- cooking spray or oil for cooking

Directions:

1. Whisk eggs and water in a bowl. Place flour in a separate shallow bowl with salt & pepper.

2. Combine both breadcrumbs, garlic powder, paprika, and salt and pepper to taste in a third bowl.

3. Toss shrimp in the flour and shake off any excess.

4. Dip in egg mixture and then into the bread crumbs gently pressing to adhere.

5. Preheat oven to 400°F (see notes for air fryer or deep fryer).

6. Spray shrimp with cooking spray until well coated. Place in a single layer on a baking sheet.

7. Bake 6 minutes. Flip shrimp and bake for an additional 6-8 minutes or until cooked through.

Notes

Smaller shrimp may need less time, larger shrimp may need more time.

Season with salt or seasoned salt after cooking.

To Air Fry

Preheat air fryer to 400°F.

Spray shrimp with cooking spray until well coated. Place in a single layer in the air fryer basket.

Air fry for 2 minutes. Flip shrimp and air fry an additional 2-3 minutes or until cooked through.

To Deep Fry

Heat deep fryer or oil to 350°F.

Add shrimp in small batches and cook 3-4 minutes or until crispy. Drain on paper towels.

Air Fryer Crab Rangoon

Servings: 15
Cooking Time: 10 Minutes

Ingredients:

- 30 Wonton Wrappers
- 7.5 oz Jalapeño Cream Cheese
- 6 oz Imitation Crab Meat chopped
- 2 tsp Soy Sauce
- 2 tsp fresh lemon juice
- 2 tbsp vegetable oil
- Duck Sauce

Directions:

1. Soften the cream cheese.

2. In a clean bowl, stir together the cream cheese, soy sauce and lemon juice.

3. Fold in the chopped crab until well blended.

4. Using the photos as a guide, fill the wontons with the filling and fold. This recipe makes about 30 Crab Rangoon.

5.   Cook the Crab Rangoon in batches in the air fryer. My basket holds about 8 at a time. There's no need to flip the Crab Rangoon.
6.   Place the Crab Rangoon in the air fryer basket in a single layer. Brush each lightly with vegetable oil. Cook at 375 degrees F for 7-8 minutes. Until the Crab Rangoon are puffed and lightly brown.
7.   Serve with Duck Sauce for dipping.
Notes
You can use real crab meat instead of imitation for a real treat!

Healthy Baked Fish Sticks With Lemon Caper Sauce
Servings: 4
Cooking Time: 15 Minutes

Ingredients:
- Lemon Caper Sauce:
- 1/4 cup fat free plain Greek yogurt
- 3 tablespoons light mayonnaise
- 1 tablespoon drained capers
- 1 tablespoon fresh minced chives
- 1 teaspoon fresh lemon juice
- 1/4 teaspoon kosher salt
- 1/8 teaspoon black pepper
- For the Fish Sticks:
- olive oil spray (I use a mister)
- 1 pound Alaskan skinless cod fillet (about 1-inch thick (thawed if frozen))
- 3 large egg whites (or 2 whole eggs)
- 1 tablespoon Dijon mustard
- 1/2 lemon (squeezed)
- 1/8 teaspoon paprika
- 1/4 teaspoon kosher salt
- 1/8 teaspoon black pepper
- For the crumbs:
- 1 cup plain or gluten-free Panko crumbs
- 1 1/2 teaspoons Old Bay seasoning
- 2 teaspoons dried parsley flakes
- 1/2 teaspoon paprika

Directions:
1.   OVEN Directions:
2.   Combine all the ingredients for the dipping sauce in a small bowl; set aside.

3.   Preheat the oven to 450°F and adjust the rack to the center position. Spray a large rimmed baking sheet with oil.
4.   Slice the fish crosswise into 2-inch long strips, about 1-inch wide.
5.   Combine egg whites, Dijon mustard, lemon juice, paprika, salt and pepper in a medium bowl.
6.   In a second bowl combine the Panko crumbs with Old Bay seasoning, dried parsley and remaining paprika.
7.   Pat fish dry with paper towels and dip the fish into the egg mixture, then into crumbs and place on the prepared baking sheet.
8.   Spray the top of the fish with oil and bake until the crumbs are golden and the fish is cooked through, about 12 minutes, or until the crumbs are golden and the fish is cooked through.
9.   AIR FRYER Directions:
10. Preheat the air fryer to 370F.
11. In batches, transfer to the air fryer basket in a single layer and cook until the crumbs are golden and the fish is cooked through, 7 to 8 minutes, turning halfway.

Air Fryer Crab Legs
Servings: 1
Cooking Time: 5 Minutes

Ingredients:
- 1 pound snow crab legs
- 1 tbsp olive oil
- 1 tsp Old Bay Seasoning
- Optional
- 2 tbsp butter melted

Directions:
1.   Lightly rinse the crab legs, being sure they don't have any leftover sand, dirt, or store packaging on them.
2.   Very lightly coat them with olive oil.
3.   Season the shells with Old Bay Seasoning, and then place the legs in the air fryer basket.
4.   Cook at 370 degrees F for 5-7 minutes, until the shells are hot to the touch.

Air-fryer Scallops

Servings: 2

Ingredients:
- 8 large (1-oz.) sea scallops, cleaned and patted very dry
- ¼ teaspoon ground pepper
- ⅛ teaspoon salt
- Cooking spray
- ¼ cup extra-virgin olive oil
- 2 tablespoons very finely chopped flat-leaf parsley
- 2 teaspoons very finely chopped capers
- 1 teaspoon finely grated lemon zest
- ½ teaspoon finely chopped garlic

Directions:
1. Sprinkle scallops with pepper and salt. Coat the basket of an air fryer with cooking spray. Place scallops in the basket and coat them with cooking spray. Place the basket in the fryer. Cook the scallops at 400°F until they reach an internal temperature of 120°F, about 6 minutes.
2. Combine oil, parsley, capers, lemon zest and garlic in a small bowl. Drizzle over the scallops.

Air Fryer Smoked Salmon Wontons

Servings: 48
Cooking Time: 5 Minutes

Ingredients:
- 1 (6 ounce) package cream cheese, softened
- 3 ounces cold-smoked salmon, finely chopped
- 1 ½ tablespoons minced capers
- 1 ½ tablespoons finely minced red onion
- 48 wonton wrappers
- water as needed
- cooking spray

Directions:
1. Combine cream cheese, salmon, capers, and red onion in a bowl. Fill a second small bowl with water.

2. Working with 6 wonton wrappers at a time, separate them out onto a clean work surface. Place 1 teaspoon of salmon mixture in the center of each wonton. Do not overfill, as the mixture may ooze out.
3. Dip your finger in the bowl of water, and lightly wet the 4 edges of each wonton wrapper. Gently fold in half diagonally to make a triangle, and seal the edges. Try not to leave excess air in the wonton, which can cause them to burst. Lightly wet the bottom of the triangle, and fold the right side over the middle, then the left side, pressing all edges to seal. Set wontons aside, covered with a damp paper towel, while you finish making the remaining wontons.
4. Preheat the air fryer to 330 degrees F (166 degrees C). Generously mist both sides of wontons with cooking spray.
5. Place as many wontons in the air fryer basket as will fit, without overcrowding.
6. Air-fry for 5 minutes, flipping halfway through. Remove to a cooling rack and let cool while you cook the remaining wontons in batches. Best served slightly warm or at room temperature.
Cook's Notes:
I have assembled these up to 8 hours ahead of time with great results. Place in a single layer, covered with a damp paper towel, inside a sealed container in the fridge until ready to air fry.
You can also freeze them uncooked. If cooking them from frozen, let sit at room temperature for 15 minutes, and add 1 minute to cook time.

Air-fryer Pretzel-crusted Catfish

Servings: 4
Cooking Time: 10 Minutes

Ingredients:
- 4 catfish fillets (6 ounces each)
- 1/2 teaspoon salt
- 1/2 teaspoon pepper
- 2 large eggs
- 1/3 cup Dijon mustard
- 2 tablespoons 2% milk
- 1/2 cup all-purpose flour

- 4 cups honey mustard miniature pretzels, coarsely crushed
- Cooking spray
- Lemon slices, optional

Directions:

1. Preheat air fryer to 325°. Sprinkle catfish with salt and pepper. Whisk eggs, mustard and milk in a shallow bowl. Place flour and pretzels in separate shallow bowls. Coat fillets with flour, then dip in egg mixture and coat with crushed pretzels.

2. In batches, place fillets in a single layer on greased tray in air-fryer basket; spritz with cooking spray. Cook until fish flakes easily with a fork, 10-12 minutes. If desired, serve with lemon slices.

Air Fryer Bang Bang Shrimp

Servings: 3-4
Cooking Time: 20 Minutes

Ingredients:
- ¾ cup mayonnaise
- ⅓ cup sweet chili sauce
- 1-3 teaspoons sriracha, or to taste
- 1 ½ pounds large shrimp, peeled and deveined, tail on
- ⅔ cup cornstarch
- ½ cup buttermilk
- 2 cups panko bread crumbs
- ½ teaspoon kosher salt

Directions:

1. In a small mixing bowl, combine mayonnaise, sweet chili sauce, and sriracha until well blended; set aside. Place the cornstarch in a plastic zipper bag or a shallow bowl. Pour the buttermilk into a separate shallow bowl. In a third shallow bowl, mix the bread crumbs and salt.

2. Preheat your air fryer to 400 degrees F.

3. Pat the shrimp dry and place them in the bag (or bowl) of cornstarch. Seal and shake the bag to coat the shrimp fully. Shake off any excess cornstarch and place the shrimp on a plate.

4. Working in batches, dredge the shrimp in buttermilk, then roll them in the breadcrumbs, pressing them firmly so the crumbs stick. Place the coated shrimp in a single layer in the air fryer, leaving a bit of space between them (you may need to work in batches). Spray them lightly with cooking spray.

5. Air fry for 5 minutes, then flip the shrimp, spray with cooking oil, and fry for another 5 minutes until the shrimp is fully cooked.

6. Transfer the cooked shrimp to a medium mixing bowl and repeat with the remaining coated shrimp.

7. When all the shrimp are cooked, pour the bang bang sauce over them and lightly toss until they are fully covered.

8. Garnish with parsley and serve immediately.

DESSERTS RECIPES

Air Fryer Prosciutto-wrapped Apples

Ingredients:
- 1 large Honeycrisp apple, cored and cut into 16-20 slices
- 3 oz. thinly sliced prosciutto
- Goat cheese, crumbled
- Arugula
- Chopped pistachios, for garnish
- Fresh thyme, for garnish
- Honey, for drizzling

Directions:
1. Start by cutting each slice of prosciutto in half. Slice the apple into about 16-20 even slices.
2. Wrap the center of the apple with prosciutto, allowing the ends of the apple to peak out.
3. Place all the wrapped apples in the air fryer basket. Cook at 400°F for about 5 minutes, or just enough to crisp up the prosciutto.
4. Transfer to a plate with a bed of arugula. Top with goat cheese, chopped pistachios, and drizzle with honey.

Air Fryer Vegan Chocolate Zucchini Birthday Cake
Servings: 4

Ingredients:
- CAKE
- 2 tbsp. neutral oil, such as avocado or vegetable, plus more for pan
- 3/4 c. all-purpose flour
- 1/2 c. vegan granulated sugar
- 3 tbsp. dark unsweetened cocoa powder
- 1 tsp. instant espresso powder
- 1/2 tsp. baking soda
- 1/4 tsp. kosher salt
- 1/2 c. almond milk creamer or regular almond milk
- 1 tsp. pure vanilla extract
- 3/4 c. shredded zucchini (from 1 small zucchini)
- 1 tbsp. apple cider vinegar
- FROSTING
- 3/4 c. vegan powdered sugar
- 2 tbsp. margarine, room temperature
- 1 tbsp. almond milk creamer or almond milk
- 1 tsp. dark unsweetened cocoa powder
- 1/2 tsp. pure vanilla extract
- Sprinkles, for serving (optional)

Directions:
1. CAKE
2. Brush a 7" nonstick round pan with oil. Line pan with parchment paper; brush parchment with oil. In a medium bowl, whisk flour, granulated sugar, cocoa powder, espresso powder, baking soda, and salt to combine. Add creamer, vanilla, and oil and stir to combine. Add zucchini and vinegar and gently fold to combine.
3. Immediately scrape batter into prepared pan, smoothing top. Place pan in an air-fryer basket. Cook at 350° until cake is puffed and a tester inserted into center comes out clean, 30 to 35 minutes.
4. Let cake cool in pan 5 minutes, then invert onto a wire rack and remove parchment. Let cool completely.
5. FROSTING
6. Using an electric mixer on medium-high speed, in a large bowl, beat powdered sugar, margarine, creamer, cocoa powder, and vanilla until smooth and fluffy, about 2 minutes.
7. Spread frosting over cake. Decorate with sprinkles, if using.

Rolling Pin Cookies
Servings: 25

Ingredients:
- 115g Butter
- 130g Light Brown Sugar
- 2 tbsp Milk
- 240g Plain Flour
- 2 tsp Baking Powder
- 1/2 tsp Bicarbonate of Soda
- 2 tsp Cinnamon
- 1/2 tsp Ground Cloves
- 1/4 tsp ground Allspice
- 1/4 tsp ground Nutmeg
- 1/4 tsp Black Pepper
- 1/2 tsp ground dried Ginger
- Pinch salt

Directions:
1. Beat the butter and sugar for a few minutes, until light and fluffy.
2. Add the milk and stir through.
3. In a bowl, combine flour, baking powder, bicarbonate of soda, cinnamon, cloves, all spice, nutmeg, black pepper, ginger, and salt.
4. Add to the butter mixture gradually. Gather dough it into a ball, flatten it into a disk, cover well and freeze for 10 minutes.
5. Roll out the dough on a floured surface with a regular rolling pin and then roll to to a quarter-inch thickness with the embossed rolling pin and cut with cookie cutters.
6. Continue to roll out and cut till all the dough is used up.
7. Preheat air fryer to180 C. Airfry for 8 – 9 minutes.
8. Remove to a wire rack and continue with remaining cookies.

Air Fryer Cake
Servings: 6-8
Cooking Time: 25 Minutes

Ingredients:
- 1 cup granulated sugar
- ¾ cup plus 2 tablespoons all-purpose flour
- ½ cup unsweetened cocoa powder
- 1 teaspoon baking powder
- ½ teaspoon baking soda
- ½ teaspoon kosher salt
- 1 large egg
- ½ cup buttermilk
- ¼ cup vegetable oil
- 1 teaspoons vanilla extract
- ½ cup boiling water

Directions:
1. Preheat your air fryer to 350 degrees F.
2. Spray the inside of a 7-inch air fryer-safe cake pan with baking spray, then line with a 9-inch round piece of parchment paper, making sure it drapes up the sides a bit. Spray with more cooking spray and set aside.
3. In a large bowl, whisk together the sugar, flour, cocoa powder, baking powder, baking soda, and salt. Add the egg, buttermilk, vegetable oil, and vanilla extract. Mix for 2 minutes, until well combined. Stir in the boiling water to create a thin batter.
4. Pour the batter into the prepared pan and place it in the air fryer basket.
5. Cook for 25 minutes, or until the cake is baked through, leaving no crumbs on an inserted toothpick. Cool in the pan for 10 minutes, then remove to a wire rack to cool completely.
6. Decorate with frosting and sprinkles, if desired.

Caramel Vanilla Cake
Servings: 4
Cooking Time: 17 Minutes

Ingredients:
- For the cake:
- 1.5 cups flour
- ¾ cup sugar
- ½ tsp bicarb
- 1 tsp baking powder
- ¼ tsp salt
- 1 egg
- ½ cup oil
- ½ cup buttermilk
- ½ cup warm water
- 2 tsp vanilla

Directions:

1. Set the Duo Crisp (with Air Fry lid) or your Vortex to Bake at 180c for 17 minutes. Allow it to pre-heat. While it heats, combine all the wet ingredients in a large bowl, once fully incorporated add the dry ingredients, mix until just combined - do not over mix! Pour the mixture into 4 greased mini loaf pans, place inside and Bake for 180c for 17 minutes. Test the cake and check if it is cooked through, use oven mits to remove carefully and allow to cool.

2. For the caramel:

3. 1 condensed milk tin

4. Pour the condensed milk into a jar and seal securely, but not too tight. Place inside the Duo Crisp or Instant Pot, on the trivet, and fill with boiling water until 4/5 of the jar is covered. Set to Pressure Cook for 30 – 50 minutes depending on the colour of caramel preferred. The longer the pressure cook, the darker the caramel. Once complete, do a Quick Release and open the lid carefully. Using oven mits, carefully lift the jar/s out and set aside to cool. Do not open until cooled. Once cooled open the lids and using a small whisk or fork stir brisky to mix well. Then spoon over the cool vanilla cakes before serving.

Air Fryer Jelly Donuts

Servings: 8
Cooking Time: 5 Minutes

Ingredients:
- 1 package Pillsbury Grands (Homestyle)
- 1/2 cup seedless raspberry jelly
- 1 tablespoon butter, melted
- 1/2 cup sugar

Directions:
1. Preheat air fryer to 320 degrees.
2. Place Grand Rolls inside the air fryer in a single layer and cook for 5-6 minutes until golden brown.
3. Remove rolls from the air fryer and set aside.
4. Place sugar into a wide bowl with a flat bottom.

5. Baste butter on all sides of the donut and roll in the sugar to cover completely. Complete with all remaining donuts.
6. Using a long cake tip, pipe 1-2 tablespoons of raspberry jelly into each donut.
7. Enjoy immediately or keep up to 3 days.*
NOTES
*donuts are best when eaten warm. If not consuming immediately, you can store the rolls after cooked. When ready to eat, reheat in a preheated air fryer at 300 degrees for 2-3 minutes then coat with butter and sugar and pipe jelly in when ready to eat.

Air Fryer Snickerdoodle Cookies

Servings: 30
Cooking Time: 8 Minutes

Ingredients:
- 3/4 cup unsalted butter
- 1 cup granulated sugar
- 1/3 cup brown sugar
- 2 large eggs
- 1 teaspoon vanilla extract
- 2 cups all purpose flour
- 1 teaspoon ground cinnamon
- 1/2 teaspoon nutmeg
- 1/2 teaspoon salt
- 1/2 teaspoon baking soda
- Cinnamon Sugar Coating
- 1/2 cup sugar
- 2 tablespoons cinnamon

Directions:
1. To make these cookies from scratch, combine the butter, sugar, and brown sugar in a large mixing bowl.
2. Using a stand or had mixer, beat the butter with sugars until smooth and creamy.
3. Add eggs, vanilla, salt, baking soda, cinnamon, nutmeg, and half of the flour. Mix until the dry ingredients combine with the butter mixture.
4. Add the remaining half of the flour mixture to the wet ingredients and mix on medium speed until the cookie dough is thick and creamy. Scrape any remaining dough

from the sides of the bowl to ensure even mixing.

5. In a small shallow bowl, combine the sugar and cinnamon for the coating, and mix.

6. Use a small cookie scoop or tablespoon to shape the equal-sized dough balls. Then gently roll the ball of dough in the bowl with cinnamon sugar mixture.

7. Place the dough in Air Fryer basket on parchment paper. Leave about an inch between dough balls. Air Fry at 300 degrees F for 8-10 minutes until edges golden brown. Allow cookies to sit in air fryer basket for an additional 1 to 2 minutes cooking time before transferring to a wire rack.

NOTES

Be careful not to overbake the cookies, or they will be tough. You want the cookies to look slightly undercooked when you pull them out to ensure they remain chewy.

To make these cookies a special dessert, place one or two in a small bowl, and top with vanilla ice cream.

This recipe makes 30-36 cookies.

Key Lime Pie Cookies

Ingredients:

- 1 cup salted butter, at room temperature
- 1 1/4 cups granulated sugar
- 1 large egg
- 1 teaspoon vanilla extract
- 3 tablespoons key lime juice
- 2 teaspoons grated lime zest
- 1/2 teaspoon Kosher salt
- 1/2 teaspoon baking soda
- 2 1/4 cups all-purpose flour
- 1 cup graham cracker crumbs, finely crushed
- 1/2 cup white chocolate chips

Directions:

1. Preheat the air fryer oven to 350F.

2. In a large bowl, mix the butter and sugar for about 2 minutes until light and fluffy.

3. Add the egg, vanilla, key lime juice and lime zest and continue mixing for 1 more

minute. Make sure to scrape down the sides of the bowl if needed.

4. Mix in the salt and baking soda until incorporated.

5. Add in the flour and graham cracker crumbs until the dough comes together.

6. Roll the dough into 1-inch balls and place 2 inches apart on the baking sheet. Bake for 15 minutes, until the edges are lightly golden.

7. Transfer the cookies to a wire rack to cool.

8. Melt the white chocolate in a microwave-safe bowl for about 30 seconds and stir. Repeat this process until the white chocolate is melted and smooth. Transfer the melted chocolate to a small sandwich bag. Snip one corner of the bag off with scissors and drizzle the white chocolate on top of the cookies.

9. Sprinkle some additional graham cracker crumbs and lime zest and enjoy!

Spiced Hot Fruit Bake

Ingredients:

- 2 cup apples, sliced
- 2 cups pears, sliced
- 1 1/2 cups fresh cranberries
- 1 cup pineapple chunks (save the juice)
- 1 Tbsp. lemon juice
- 1/2 stick butter, melted
- 1/3 cup brown sugar
- 1/4 tsp nutmeg
- 1 tsp cinnamon
- 1 Tbsp. honey, maple syrup, or agave
- 1/3 cup chopped raw walnuts or pecans
- Extra cinnamon and nuts, for serving

Directions:

1. Preheat Air Fryer Oven to 350F.

2. In a large bowl, toss apples, pears, cranberries and pineapples and the 1 Tbsp. lemon juice. Set aside.

3. In another glass bowl, combine your melted butter, nutmeg, cinnamon, honey and a little bit of the leftover pineapple juice (about 1 Tablespoon).

4. Add this sugar/butter mixture to your fruit and coat evenly.

5. Pour fruit into a 8×8 baking dish and sprinkle the chopped pecans and walnuts on top.
6. Bake for about 45 minutes, stirring throughout.
7. Serve over ice cream and enjoy the best holiday sundae! Sprinkle any additional cinnamon and nuts over the top, if desired.

Air-fryer Cheesecake
Servings: 10
Cooking Time: 35 Minutes

Ingredients:
- 125g plain sweet biscuits, broken into pieces
- 60g unsalted butter, melted
- 750g cream cheese, softened
- 1 tsp vanilla extract
- 2/3 cup caster sugar
- 3 free range eggs
- 1/4 cup sour cream
- 125g raspberries
- 2 tbs maple syrup

Directions:
1. Grease a 19cm-round springform pan. Line side with baking paper, ensuring paper doesn't extend over the edge of pan.
2. Place biscuits in a food processor. Process until fine crumbs form. Add butter. Process until just combined. Press biscuit mixture over base of prepared pan. Refrigerate for 30 minutes.
3. Meanwhile, wash and dry food processor. Process cream cheese, vanilla and sugar until smooth. Add egg and sour cream. Process until just combined. Pour mixture into prepared pan.
4. Cover pan with foil. Place pan into the basket of a 12-litre air fryer. Set temperature to 180°C and cook cheesecake for 30 minutes. Uncover and cook for a further 5 minutes or until top is golden. Turn air fryer off and allow cheesecake to stand in air fryer for 30 minutes to cool. Remove from air fryer and refrigerate overnight. Serve topped with raspberry and drizzled with maple syrup.

Air Fryer Cherry Pie Taquitos
Servings: 4
Cooking Time: 6 Minutes

Ingredients:
- 1 can cherry pie filling 21-ounce
- 12 medium soft flour tortillas
- 4 tablespoons butter melted
- 2 teaspoons powdered sugar optional

Directions:
1. Lay tortillas flat, and then spoon about 2 tablespoons of filling across the center of the tortilla. Roll tightly.
2. Brush the rolled taquito with melted butter.
3. Place in the air fryer basket, seam side down, without stacking or overlapping.
4. Air fry at 350 degrees F for 9-11 minutes, until the taquito is golden and crispy.
5. One can makes about 6 taquitos. Don't overfill-you should be able to roll it tightly.
6. Sprinkle with powdered sugar and serve.
NOTES
Add toppings - Let's be real and talk about the fact that toppings can make everything better. Adding a bit of cinnamon sugar mixture on top is the perfect sweet addition. You can also drizzle caramel sauce, sprinkle brown sugar, or top with some fresh fruit.
Change the fruit filling - I'm a fan of fruit pies, and this recipe makes it easy to change things up. If you want to give the cherry filling a break, try and make it again using blueberry pie filling, apple pie filling, or even fresh apples in this decadent dessert.

Steamed Hot Cross Bun Cake
Servings: 4-6
Cooking Time: 35 Minutes

Ingredients:
- 1 pkt hot cross buns
- 3 TBSP Butter
- 4 Eggs
- ½ cup Milk
- Pinch salt
- 5ml vanilla essence
- 1 tsp Cinnamon

- 1/3 cup Brown sugar

Directions:
1. Slice the hot cross buns and spread each slice generously with butter.
2. Arrange the slices in the greased solid based cake pan (18 – 20cm depending on size of your Instant Pot).
3. Whisk the eggs, milk, salt & vanilla essence together and pour over the hot cross buns.
4. Allow to stand for 5 mins.
5. Cover the pan tightly with foil.
6. Pour 1 cup of water into the inner pot and place the trivet inside.
7. Place the pan on the trivet and secure the lid.
8. Set to Pressure Cook on High for 12 mins then allow 15 mins Natural Release and then Quick release remaining pressure.
9. Once pin drops, open lid and remove the pan. Dry off with paper towels and remove foil.
10. Sprinkle the cake with cinnamon and sugar.
11. Set the Vortex to Bake at 180c for 5 mins.
12. Serve with whipped cream or ice cream.

Air Fryer Pumpkin Spice Muffins
Servings: 12
Cooking Time: 12 Minutes

Ingredients:
- 1 cup flour
- 1 teaspoon baking powder
- ⅓ cup sugar
- 1 teaspoon vanilla extract
- 1 tablespoon pumpkin spice
- ⅓ cup pumpkin puree
- 1 egg
- ¼ cup milk
- 3 tablespoon oil

Directions:
1. Preheat air fryer to 360°F on bake.
2. Place muffin liners into a muffin tray. Set aside.
3. In a bowl combine flour, baking powder and sugar. In another bowl combine vanilla extract, pumpkin spice, pumpkin puree, egg, milk and oil.
4. Slowly mix wet ingredients into dry ingredients, whipping until everything is well incorporated and there are no lumps.
5. Divide the batter between the muffin liners, place it in the air fryer basket.
6. Bake for 10-12 minutes or until a toothpick comes out clean from the centre of the muffin.
Notes
Store in an airtight container for 2-3 days on the counter or freeze in a zippered bag for up to 3 months.

Blueberry & Lemon Muffins
Servings: 12

Ingredients:
- 200g self-raising flour
- 1 tsp baking powder
- 1/2 tsp salt
- Zest of 1 lemon
- 125g golden caster sugar
- 100ml vegetable oil
- 100ml natural yogurt
- 2 large eggs, beaten
- 100g blueberries

Directions:
1. Sift the flour, baking powder and salt into a large mixing bowl. Make a well in center
2. Mix in lemon, sugar, oil, yogurt, eggs and continue stirring together until the oil is incorporated. Stir in blueberries
3. Insert crisper plate in both drawers
4. Place 4-6 double thickness muffin cases in each drawer (depending on size of muffin case), spoon mixture between the muffin cases. Select zone 1, select BAKE, set temperature to 160°C, and set time to 20 minutes. Select MATCH. Press the START/STOP button to begin cooking
5. After 15 minutes, check whether muffins are cooked through. Cooking is complete when a wooden skewer inserted in the center comes out clean. Remove muffins from drawer and let cool on a wire rack for 5 minutes before serving

Air Fryer Banana Blueberry Muffins

Servings: 14

Ingredients:

- 3/4 c. all-purpose flour
- 3/4 c. whole wheat flour
- 1 tsp. baking powder
- 1 tsp. baking soda
- 1/4 tsp. kosher salt
- 3 large overripe bananas
- 1 large egg
- 3/4 c. packed light brown sugar
- 1/3 c. vegetable oil
- 1/4 c. sour cream
- 1 tsp. pure vanilla extract
- 1 c. fresh or frozen blueberries (unthawed if frozen)
- 14 banana chips

Directions:

1. In a medium bowl, whisk all-purpose flour, whole wheat flour, baking powder, baking soda, and salt.
2. In a large bowl, mash bananas witha fork. Add egg, brown sugar, oil, sour cream, and vanilla and whisk to combine.
3. Add dry ingredients to wet ingredients and stir until just combined. Fold in blueberries.
4. Scoop batter with a 2.5-oz. scoop or 1/3-cup measuring cup into 14 silicone muffin liners. Top with 1 banana chip.
5. Working in batches, in an air-fryer basket, arrange filled muffin liners, spacing about 1/2" apart. Cook at 350° for 7 minutes. Tent tops with foil to prevent overbrowning, then continue to cook until puffed and a tester inserted into center comes out clean, 5 to 7 minutes more.
6. Transfer muffins to a wire rack and let cool.

Air Fryer Blackberry & Apple Crumble

Servings: 6
Cooking Time: 1 Hour

Ingredients:

- 1kg Bramley apples (about 4-6), peeled, cored and cut into 2cm chunks
- 200g blackberries
- 50g caster sugar
- ½ lemon, zest and juice
- vanilla ice cream, custard or double cream, to server
- Crumble
- 150g plain flour
- 100g chilled unsalted butter, cubed
- 75g caster sugar
- 50g porridge oats
- ½ tsp ground cinnamon

Directions:

1. First, make the crumble. In a medium bowl, use your fingertips to gently rub all the ingredients together until evenly combined (you'll have mostly small chunks with a few larger ones) and put in the fridge. .
2. Put the apple chunks and blackberries in the base of the air-fryer basket (without the rack). Toss through the sugar, lemon zest and juice, and 2 tbsp water with a pinch of salt; spread out evenly.
3. Scrunch the chilled crumble mix together then loosely scatter over the fruit to cover (this will help give you different-sized crumble pieces). Air-fry at 180ºC for 1 hour, covering with foil after 25 minutes if needed, until golden and well cooked and the fruit is very tender and piping hot. Serve immediately with ice cream, custard or cream.

NOTES
Customer safety tips
Follow manufacturer's instructions and advice for specific foods
Pre-heat the air fryer to the correct temperature
If cooking different foods together, be aware that they may require different times and temperatures
Spread food evenly – do not overcrowd pan/chamber
Turn food midway through cooking
Check food is piping/steaming hot and cooked all the way through
Aim for golden colouring – do not overcook

Air Fryer Donuts With Biscuits

Servings: 8
Cooking Time: 5 Minutes

Ingredients:
- 16 oz refrigerated flaky jumbo biscuits
- 1/2 c. granulated white sugar
- 2 tsp ground cinnamon
- 4 Tbsp butter melted
- olive or coconut oil spray

Directions:
1. Combine sugar and cinnamon in a shallow bowl; set aside.
2. Remove the biscuits from the can, separate them and place them on a flat surface. Use a 1-inch round biscuit cutter (or similarly-sized bottle cap) to cut holes out of the center of each biscuit.
3. Lightly coat air fryer basket with olive or coconut oil spray. Do not use non-stick spray like Pam because it can damage the coating on the basket.
4. Place 4 donuts in a single layer in the air fryer basket. Make sure they are not touching.
5. Air Fry at 360 degrees F for 5 minutes or until lightly browned.
6. Remove donuts from Air Fryer, dip in melted butter then roll in cinnamon sugar to coat. Serve immediately.

Air Fryer Cranberry Brie Bites

Ingredients:
- 1 – 8 oz. tube crescent dough
- 1 – 8 oz. wheel of brie cheese
- 1 cup whole berry cranberry sauce
- rosemary sprigs, fresh
- all-purpose flour, for sprinkling

Directions:
1. Preheat your air fryer to 375°F. Spray your air fryer safe muffin tin with cooking spray and set aside.
2. Spread a little flour out onto your counter. Then, roll out the crescent dough and pinch the seams together. Cut the crescent roll dough into 14 equal sized squares. Place the squares into the muffin tin slots.
3. Cut the brie cheese into small pieces and place inside the crescent dough squares. Top with a generous spoonful of cranberry sauce and a little sprig of rosemary.
4. Place the muffin tin into your air fryer and bake for 5-7 minutes, or until the crescent dough is a light golden brown.

Baked Apple Chips

Servings: 4
Cooking Time: 2 Hours 30 Minutes

Ingredients:
- 3 gala apples

Directions:
1. Preheat oven to 200 F. Line a large 1/2 pan baking sheet with a slipat mat or parchment paper.
2. From the bottom of the apples, slice into very thin slices, about 1/8 thick. Use a mandoline or a knife to slice. Place them down in a single even layer on the lined baking pan. You don't need to leave any space between them as they will shrink. For extra flavour, you can sprinkle some cinnamon on top.
3. Bake for 1 hour, then flip the apple slices over and bake for another 1.5 hours. If the apples aren't crispy enough, continue to bake, checking on them every 10-15 minutes.
NOTES
Equipment used: mandoline slicer, half sheet baking pan, and silpat liner.
How to cook in the air fryer: Preheat the air fryer to 200 F, about 3 minutes. Place apple slices in a single layer in the air fryer basket and air fry for 20 minutes until crispy.
How to slice apples super thin: I use a mandoline slicer on the thinest setting to slice the apples super thin and evenly. You can also use a knife. You want to slice the apples about 1/8-inch thick
How to make apple cinnamon chips: You can switch things up and add a little cinnamon on top for a different flavour. You can sprinkle about a teaspoon on cinnamon on top before popping the apples into the oven.

How to store: Store homemade apple chips in an airtight container for up to 1 week at room temperature.

Pumpkin Biscuits

Ingredients:
- Biscuits:
- ¾ cup pumpkin puree
- ½ cup sugar, divided
- 1 tsp vanilla extract
- 1 tsp pumpkin pie spice
- 1 can Pillsbury Grands biscuits, 8 count
- 1 tsp cinnamon
- Glaze:
- ½ cup powdered sugar
- 1 tsp cinnamon
- 3 tbsp heavy whipping cream or milk

Directions:
1. Spray an air fryer safe baking pan with nonstick cooking spray.
2. In a mixing bowl, combine the pumpkin puree, ¼ cup sugar, vanilla and pumpkin pie spice, stirring thoroughly. Set aside.
3. Open the can of biscuits and slice each in half horizontally. In a small bowl, stir together the remaining ¼ cup sugar and cinnamon. Then, coat each biscuit half with the cinnamon sugar mixture.
4. Lay one slice of dough flat. Spread the pumpkin mixture on top and place another biscuit on top. Place the biscuits in the baking pan.
5. Carefully place the baking pan in the Air Fryer Oven and bake at 350°F for 15 minutes, or until the top is golden and the center is cooked through.
6. While you are waiting for the biscuits to cook, prepare the glaze. In a small bowl, whisk together the powdered sugar, cinnamon and heavy whipping cream until a smooth sauce forms.
7. Carefully take the baking pan out of the Air Fryer Oven and let cool before glazing. Once you have waited, drizzle over the biscuits, pull apart and serve!

Air Fryer Cinnamon Sugar Dessert Fries

Servings: 4
Cooking Time: 15 Minutes

Ingredients:
- 2 sweet potatoes
- 1 tablespoon butter, melted
- 1 teaspoon butter, melted and separated from the above
- 2 tablespoons sugar
- 1/2 teaspoon cinnamon

Directions:
1. Preheat your air fryer to 380 degrees.
2. Peel and cut the sweet potatoes into skinny fries
3. Coat fries with 1 tablespoon of butter.
4. Cook fries in the preheated air fryer for 15-18 minutes. They can overlap, but should not fill your air fryer more than 1/2 full.
5. Remove the sweet potato fries from the air fryer and place them in a bowl.
6. Coat with the remaining butter and add in sugar and cinnamon. Mix to coat.
7. Enjoy immediately.

Air Fryer Caramelized Bananas Bananas

Servings: 12
Cooking Time: 6 Minutes

Ingredients:
- 2 bananas
- ¼ of a lemon, juiced
- 1 tablespoon coconut sugar
- optonal toppings: cinnamon, nuts, coconut cream, yogurt, granola... etc.

Directions:
1. Wash your bananas with the peel on, then slice them straight down the middle, length wise
2. Squeeze lemon juice over top of each banana
3. If using cinnamon mix with in with the coconut sugar, then sprinkle over top of the bananas until coated

4. Place into parchment lined air fryer for 6-8 minutes at 400F
5. Once taken out of the airfryer, eat as is or top with your favourite toppings and enjoy!

Apple Chips
Servings: 2

Ingredients:
- 2 apples, thinly sliced
- 2 tsp. granulated sugar
- 1/2 tsp. cinnamon

Directions:
1. FOR OVEN
2. Preheat oven to 200°. In a large bowl, toss apples with sugar and cinnamon.
3. Place a metal rack inside a rimmed baking sheet. Lay apples slices on top of rack, spacing them so that no apples overlap.
4. Bake for 2 to 3 hours, flipping apples halfway through, until apples dried out but still pliable. (Apples will continue to crisp while cooling.)
5. FOR AIR FRYER
6. In a large bowl toss apples with cinnamon and sugar. Working in batches, place apples in a single layer in basket of air fryer (some overlap is okay).
7. Bake at 350° for about 12 minutes, flipping every 4 minutes.

Air Fryer Apples
Servings: 2
Cooking Time: 12 Minutes

Ingredients:
- 2 red apples, pink lady, honey crisp, or gala, peeled, cored, and cut into 1-inch bite-sized cubes
- 2 Tbsp real maple syrup, divided
- 1 Tbsp melted coconut oil, refined has no taste
- 1 tsp cinnamon

Directions:
1. Preheat your air fryer to 380°F and lightly spray with non-stick spray.
2. Add the peeled apple cubes into a bowl and toss with 1 Tablespoon maple syrup, coconut oil, and cinnamon.

3. Add apple cubes to the heated air fryer basket. Make sure they don't overlap too much, or else they will not cook properly.
4. Air fry for 10 - 14 minutes, shaking halfway through. They should be golden, slightly crispy on the outside, and tender on the inside.
5. Remove from the air fryer and toss the warm apples in 1 Tablespoon of maple syrup.
6. Enjoy warm with vanilla ice cream, oatmeal, or on its own!
Notes
Maple Syrup: I highly reccomend using maple syrup, but you can substitute with honey if needed.
Coconut Oil: Use refined coconut oil for no coconut taste. You can also substitute with olive oil if needed.
Storing: They are best enjoyed within 20 minutes of air frying, but you can also store leftovers in an airtight container in the fridge for up to 4 days.
Reheating: Reheat in a microwave-safe bowl for 30 - 45 seconds until warm.

Air Fryer Goat Cheese Balls
Servings: 4
Cooking Time: 8 Minutes

Ingredients:
- 8 oz goat cheese
- 1/4 cup flour
- 1 large egg beaten
- 1/2 cup panko breadcrumbs
- olive oil spray
- Garnish:
- honey
- thyme

Directions:
1. Divide the goat cheese into 12 pieces and roll into balls. Place on a plate and put in the freezer for 20 minutes.
2. While the goat cheese balls are in the freezer, create the dredging stations: one for flour, one for the beaten egg, and one for the breadcrumbs.
3. Remove the goat cheese balls from the freezer and one by one, dredge in the flour, then the beaten egg, then the breadcrumbs. Once the goat cheese balls have finished with

the dredging station, place on a plate or sheet pan and spray with a light coat of olive oil.

4. Place the goat cheese balls on a single layer in the air fryer and cook at 370 F for 6 to 8 minutes, until they are golden.

5. Drizzle some honey over them and garnish with thyme and serve immediately.

Air Fryer Chocolate Chip Cookies

Servings: 2

Ingredients:
- Deselect All
- 1 1/4 cups all-purpose flour (see Cook's Note)
- 1/4 teaspoon baking soda
- 1/4 teaspoon fine salt
- 1/4 cup granulated sugar
- 1/4 cup packed light brown sugar
- 4 tablespoons unsalted butter, at room temperature
- 1 large egg
- 1 teaspoon pure vanilla extract
- 1/2 cup semi-sweet chocolate chips

Directions:
1. Set air fryer to 325 F. Cut out a piece of parchment that just covers the bottom of the air fryer insert.

2. Whisk together the flour, baking soda and salt in a medium bowl.

3. Beat together both of the sugars and the butter in another bowl with an electric hand mixer on medium-high speed until light and fluffy, about 3 minutes. Scrap down the bowl with a rubber spatula. Beat in the egg and then the vanilla. Reduce mixer speed to low, add the flour mixture and beat until just combined. Stir in the chocolate chips with a wooden spoon.

4. Scoop out slightly heaping tablespoonfuls of dough and roll into balls. Working in batches (about 6 at a time), arrange them at least 1 inch apart on the parchment-lined insert. Air-fry until golden brown, 6 to 8 minutes. Let cool in the insert for a couple minutes and then transfer with a spatula to a wire rack and cool completely. Cook the remaining dough balls in batches.

Notes
When measuring flour, we spoon it into a dry measuring cup and level off the excess. (Scooping directly from the bag compacts the flour, resulting in dry baked goods.)

Sesame Seed Balls

Servings: 4-5

Ingredients:
- 9 ounces red bean paste
- 2 cups glutinous rice flour
- 2 tablespoons wheat starch
- ½ cup granulated sugar
- A pinch kosher salt
- 1 teaspoon toasted sesame oil
- 1½ tablespoons canola oil, plus more for hands
- ¾ cup warm water
- ½ cup white sesame seeds

Directions:
1. Divide the red bean paste into nine 1-ounce balls. Place in the fridge for 5 minutes.

2. Whisk together rice flour, wheat starch, sugar, and kosher salt in a large bowl until well combined.

3. Whisk in the sesame oil and 1½ tablespoons of canola oil into the flour mixture.

4. Stir in the warm water until a dough forms.

5. Knead the dough until smooth, about 2 minutes.

6. Divide the dough into 9 equal balls and lightly coat with canola oil.

7. Flatten the dough balls into 3-inch circles and place a red bean paste ball in the center.

8. Pinch the edges of the dough together to cover the red bean ball and roll to make a ball.

9. Roll each ball into white sesame seeds.

10. Select the Preheat function on the Air Fryer, adjust to 350°F, and press Start/Pause.

11. Place the sesame seed balls into the preheated air fryer basket lined with parchment paper.

12. Adjust the temperature to 350°F, set time to 25 minutes, and press Start/Pause.

13. Remove from the air fryer and allow it to cool before serving or enjoy hot.

SALADS & SIDE DISHES RECIPES

Air-fryer Nuggets Lunch Boxes

Servings: 4
Cooking Time: 20 Minutes

Ingredients:
- 4 slices Woolworths wholemeal bread, toasted
- 2 small carrots, grated
- 150g chicken mince
- 1 free range egg
- 5ml olive oil cooking spray
- 1 large Lebanese cucumber, cut into batons
- 80g light tasty cheese, diced
- 4 kiwi fruit, cut into wedges

Directions:
1. Preheat air fryer on 200°C for 4 minutes. Meanwhile, place bread into a food processor. Process for 15 seconds until fine crumbs form. Transfer to a bowl and set aside.
2. Place carrot in food processor. Process for 15 seconds or until finely chopped. Add chicken, egg and half of the breadcrumbs. Season with pepper. Pulse for 10 seconds or until just combined. Using damp hands, form tablespoonfuls of the chicken mixture into nuggets, then coat in remaining breadcrumbs.
3. Spray half the nuggets with oil and place, in a single layer, in air-fryer basket. Cook for 8 minutes, turning halfway, or until golden and cooked through. Repeat with remaining nuggets and oil. Serve nuggets in lunch boxes with cucumber, cheese and kiwi fruit.

Air Fryer Chimichangas

Servings: 4
Cooking Time: 10 Minutes

Ingredients:
- 1 tbsp unsalted butter melted
- ¼ cup onion diced
- 1 cup shredded chicken cooked
- 4 ounces cream cheese softened
- 3 tsp taco seasoning
- 1 cup mexican cheese blend shredded
- ¼ tsp ground black pepper
- 4 flour tortillas 8-inch

Directions:
1. Preheat the air fryer to 400 degrees Fahrenheit.
2. In a small bowl, combine the onion, chicken, cream cheese, taco seasoning, Mexican blend cheese, and ground black pepper. Mix well.
3. Brush one side of each tortilla with butter. Place the butter side down. Scoop 3 Tablespoons of chicken mixture into the center of the tortilla. Fold the tortilla in and roll it closed, then secure it with a toothpick.
4. Repeat for the remainder of the tortillas.
5. Place the chimichangas in a single layer in the basket of the air fryer. Air fry at 400 degrees Fahrenheit for 4 minutes, flip, and air fry for an additional 2 minutes.
6. Remove the toothpicks and serve with your favorite dipping sauce.
NOTES
I make this recipe in my Cosori 5.8 qt. air fryer or 6.8 quart air fryer. Depending on your air fryer, size and wattages, cooking time may need to be adjusted 1-2 minutes.
Store remainder chimichangas in the refrigerator in an airtight container for up to 3 days.

Buffalo Chicken Salad

Servings: 2
Cooking Time: 0 Minutes

Ingredients:
- 6 1/2 ounces cooked chicken breast or canned (from an 8 oz breast, cubed)
- 1/4 cup red onion (plus more for garnish)
- 1/2 celery stalk (plus leaves for garnish)
- 1 baby carrot
- 1/4 cup mayo
- 1/4 cup Frank's hot sauce (or more to taste)

- 6 baby romaine lettuce leaves (or your favorite lettuce for wraps)
- light blue cheese dressing (optional for topping)

Directions:
1. If you need to cook the chicken in the slow cooker, cover it with water 4 hours on low then shred. Use a rotisserie chicken breast or even canned chicken works here.
2. In a mini chopper, chop all the veggies, then add the chicken and pulse a few times.
3. Transfer to a bowl and mix with the mayo and hot sauce, adding more to taste.
4. To serve, spoon into lettuce wraps and garnish with red onion, celery leaves and more hot sauce.

Air Fryer Roasted Garlic
Servings: 1
Cooking Time: 19 Minutes

Ingredients:
- 1 garlic bulb
- 1 tablespoon olive oil

Directions:
1. On a cutting board with a sharp knife carefully slice off the bottom part of whole head of garlic.
2. Place the fresh garlic head on a piece of aluminum foil.
3. Use a pastry brush to coat the entire bulb of garlic with olive oil or drizzle olive oil over bulb and gently roll bulb of garlic in aluminum foil to cover bulb evenly.
4. Next pull all edges of aluminum foil over garlic head. Sealing all exposed parts of bulb.
5. Air fry at 380 degrees F for 20-25 minutes, air fry until garlic softens and is golden brown.
6. Allow garlic to cool prior to removing individual garlic cloves. The best way to remove each clove of garlic is to gently squeeze top of bulb and they will easily slide out of garlic bulb.
NOTES
Optional seasonings after cooking: Pinch of salt & pepper, parmesan cheese, hand grated loose cheese, red pepper flakes, onion or garlic powder. Fresh herbs like chopped rosemary, thyme or dill will add a brightness to this recipe.

Air Fryer Egg Salad
Servings: 4
Cooking Time: 15 Minutes

Ingredients:
- 8 large eggs
- 4 tablespoons mayonnaise
- 1 tablespoon finely chopped chives or scallions (plus more for garnish)
- 1/4 teaspoon kosher salt
- fresh black pepper (to taste)
- 1/8 teaspoon sweet paprika (for garnish)

Directions:
1. Place the eggs in the air fryer basket and set the temperature to 250°F.
2. Cook for 15 to 16 minutes, depending on your air fryer until the eggs are hard-boiled (time may vary depending on the make and model of your air fryer), play around with 1 egg to see how your air fryer cooks before making a whole batch.
3. Once the eggs are cooked, remove them from the air fryer and run under cold water.
4. Peel the eggs and chop them into small pieces.
5. In a separate bowl, mix together the mayonnaise, salt, and pepper.
6. Add the chopped eggs, chives to the bowl with the mayonnaise mixture. Stir until everything is well combined.
7. Top with paprika and chives, for garnish.
8. Serve the egg salad on top of your favorite bread, crackers, or lettuce leaves, or use it to make a sandwich. Enjoy!

Air Fryer Artichoke

Servings: 4
Cooking Time: 15 Minutes

Ingredients:

- 2 medium artichoke
- 1 Tablespoon lemon juice fresh
- 1 Tablespoon olive oil
- 1 teaspoon kosher salt
- 1/2 teaspoon ground black pepper

Directions:

1. Rinse and clean the artichokes.
2. Remove outer leaves, cut the tips and shorten the stem with a sharp knife or kitchen scissors.
3. Cut them in half, lengthwise, and turn the artichoke halves so they are flat side up.
4. Place them in a baking dish.
5. Drizzle fresh lemon juice generously over entire artichoke half.
6. Next drizzle all 4 halves with olive oil, then season with salt and pepper.
7. Place each halved artichoke in air fryer basket, in a single layer, flat side down.
8. Air fry artichokes at 340 degrees F for 12-15 minutes until cooked (a knife should be able to cut through the flesh easily and they will have soft leaves).
9. Serve artichokes while hot.
NOTES
This recipe was made in a 1700 watt 5.8 quart Cosori air fryer. All air fryers can cook a little differently depending on the wattage and size. Use this recipe as a guide for best results if you are using a different air fryer.
Optional Favorite Dipping Sauce: Lemony garlic aioli sauce, feta dip, honey mustard, ranch dressing, pepper garlic aioli dip, Greek yogurt with fresh dill or ancho chili aioli.
Creamy Dipping Sauce: In a medium bowl measure 1 cup of mayonnaise with any spices, citrus juices, vinegars or herbs that you are craving.
Kitchen Tips: You can also use kitchen shears or a serrated knife to cut the artichokes. You may have to cook artichokes in batches depending on the size.

Substitutions: Avocado oil, grapeseed oil or refined coconut oil. Use a few tablespoons lemon juice to make artichokes extra tangy.

Teriyaki Root Vegetable Salad With Crispy Tofu

Servings: 2
Cooking Time: 10-30 Minutes

Ingredients:

- For the teriyaki dressing
- 60ml/2¼fl oz dark soy sauce
- 2 tbsp honey
- 1 tbsp sesame oil
- 1 tbsp rice vinegar or white wine vinegar
- 1 tsp cornflour
- 2 garlic cloves, crushed
- For the salad
- 200g/7oz firm tofu, cut into 2cm/¾in cubes and patted dry with kitchen paper
- 1 tbsp olive oil
- 1 tbsp cornflour
- 300g/10½oz celeriac, julienned
- 2 carrots, julienned
- 1 parsnip, julienned
- 100g/3½oz kale, stems removed and leaves torn
- pinch sesame seeds
- salt

Directions:

1. Preheat the oven to 200C/180C Fan/Gas 6 and put a baking tray on the middle shelf to heat up. (Or see Recipe Tip for air fryer instructions)
2. To make the dressing, whisk all of the ingredients together in a small saucepan, then bring to the boil. Cook for 2 minutes until thick and glossy, then remove from the heat and leave to cool.
3. Put the tofu in a large bowl, add 1 tablespoon of the dressing and drizzle over the olive oil. Stir to coat. Sprinkle over the cornflour, stir again, then tip onto the preheated baking tray. Roast for 25 minutes, turning halfway through cooking.
4. Meanwhile, tip the vegetables into a large bowl, add a pinch of salt and massage together

for a couple of minutes – this helps to soften them, and in turn soak up more dressing. Once the vegetables are soft, pour in 3–4 tablespoons of the dressing and toss to coat.

5. Divide the salad between 2 serving bowls, top with the crispy tofu and sprinkle over the sesame seeds.

NOTES

Use a julienne peeler to shred the vegetables. They are relatively cheap and make prepping salads like this really easy. If you don't have one you can grate the vegetables.

Plan ahead and prepare the tofu the night before. Cut into cubes, pat dry, then sandwich between a few sheets of kitchen paper. Weigh down with a plate on top and chill overnight. The more moisture you can remove in advance, the crispier the tofu will be.

You can cook the tofu in an air fryer. Just coat in cornflour then drizzle or spray with oil and air fry for 10 minutes at 180C.

Any leftover dressing will keep for up to a week in an airtight container in the fridge.

Air Fryer Portobello Mushroom

Servings: 3-4
Cooking Time: 12 Minutes

Ingredients:

- 3 to 4 portobello mushroom caps
- Juice and zest of 1 lemon
- ¼ cup parsley, loosely packed
- ¼ cup oregano, loosely packed
- 2 tablespoons loosely packed thyme
- 1 tablespoon garlic, minced
- 3 tablespoons olive oil, divided

Directions:

1. Preheat your air fryer to 350 degrees.
2. Remove the stem from your mushroom cap by carefully pulling the cap to the side and it will pop out.
3. Hold your mushroom cap under slowly running water and gently rub to remove any dirt from the outside and inside of the cap. Pat them dry with paper towels.
4. Zest your lemon with a zester or grater. Then cut your lemon in half to juice it.
5. Wash your herbs and pat them dry.

6. In a small food processor or blender, place your herbs, garlic, lemon zest and juice, and olive oil. Blend until smooth.
7. Using a basting brush, brush the mushrooms on the top and bottom till they are covered.
8. Place the mushroom caps top side down and cook at 350 degrees F for 10 minutes. Then flip the caps for an additional 2 minutes.

Air Fryer Lemon Pepper Wings

Servings: 4
Cooking Time: 20 Minutes

Ingredients:

- 24 drummies
- 1 Tablespoon olive oil
- 1 Tablespoon cornstarch
- 1 teaspoon smoked paprika
- 1 teaspoon ground black pepper
- 1 teaspoon lemon pepper
- 1/2 teaspoon lemon zest

Directions:

1. Preheat the Air Fryer to 380° Fahrenheit. Prepare the Air Fryer basket with olive oil spray.
2. Rinse and pat the wings with paper towels until they are completely dry.
3. Add the chicken wings, olive oil, cornstarch, ground black pepper, paprika, lemon pepper seasoning, and lemon zest to a large Ziploc bag.
4. Seal the bag and toss to coat the wings with the oil and seasonings.
5. Place wings in a single layer in the basket of your Air Fryer.
6. Cook at 380°F for 16 minutes, flipping every 4 minutes. Increase the heat to 400°F and cook for an additional 4 minutes. Use a meat thermometer to ensure the wings have reached 165°F. Add 1-2 minutes at 400°F if needed.
7. Remove the crispy wings from the Air Fryer basket and place them on a serving dish.
8. Serve with your favorite dipping sauce and sides.

NOTES

If you don't have cornstarch, you can use flour instead! Just make sure to use twice as much flour as cornstarch for best results.

If you're cutting up whole wings, cut off the small wing tip, and then use a sharp knife to cut the wings in the joint to make the wings and drummettes.

If you want some added lemon flavor, squeeze a little lemon juice on the wings just before serving.

Fried Eggplant With Spicy Goat Cheese Dip

Air Fryer Tempeh

Servings: 3
Cooking Time: 14 Minutes

Ingredients:

- 1- 8 ounce package of Tempeh
- ½ cup of your favorite BBQ Sauce
- 2 tablespoon of olive oil

Directions:

1. Cut your Tempeh into ½ inch strips. Then turn them on their side to cut again, making thinner strips.
2. Tempeh is fermented soy and can be bitter. To help make them tender and to take some of the bitterness away you will want to steam your tempeh before air frying it. To do this fill a pot with about 2 inches of water in it. Bring it to a boil. Place your tempeh in a steaming basket and steam for 10 minutes. If you do not have a steaming basket, you can place it in the water and hard boil it for 10 minutes, but you will need to pat them dry before the next step.
3. Preheat your air fryer to 380 degrees.
4. Place your steamed tempeh on a cutting board and brush both sides of it with olive oil. Brush the inside of your air fryer with olive oil as well. Then place your tempeh in the basket, leaving a little room around each of them.
5. Cook for 7 minutes and then flip them. Place them back in the air fryer for 4 more minutes and then remove the basket. Brush the tops of your tempeh with BBQ sauce and then place it back in the air fryer for an additional 3 minutes. (14 minutes total) This allows that BBQ sauce to caramelize and get a delicious sticky texture to it.
6. When they are cooked and are crispy, then place them back on the cutting board and brush them with BBQ sauce again, covering them. Enjoy immediately.

NOTES
HOW TO REHEAT TEMPEH IN THE AIR FRYER:
Preheat your air fryer to 350 degrees.
Place tempeh in your air fryer and cook for 3-4 minutes or until warmed thoroughly.
Brush with additional BBQ sauce if desired and serve.

Green Goddess Carrot Salad

Servings: 4

Ingredients:

- 1 lb. slim baby carrots, trimmed and cut lengthwise in half (or in quarters if large)
- 1 tbsp. olive oil
- 1 c. Green Goddess Dressing
- 1 head Bibb lettuce, leaves separated and torn
- GREEN GODDESS DRESSING
- 3/4 c. buttermilk
- 1/2 c. mayonnaise
- 1/3 c. plain Greek yogurt
- 4 anchovies or 2 tsp. anchovy paste
- 2 tbsp. fresh lemon juice
- 1 tbsp. Dijon mustard
- 1 small clove garlic
- Pinch of sugar
- 3/4 tsp. salt
- 1/4 tsp. pepper
- 1/2 c. loosely packed fresh parsley
- 1/4 c. packed fresh basil
- 3 tbsp. fresh tarragon
- 2 tbsp. snipped fresh chives

Directions:

1. Heat air fryer to 400°F. Toss carrots with 1 tablespoon olive oil and 1/2 teaspoon salt. Add carrots to air-fryer basket and air-fry until crisp-tender and edges are slightly

caramelized, 15 to 17 minutes. Cool completely.

2. Meanwhile, prepare Green Goddess Dressing: In blender, puree buttermilk, mayonnaise, Greek yogurt, anchovies or anchovy paste, lemon juice, Dijon mustard, garlic, pinch sugar, salt and pepper until smooth. Add parsley, basil, tarragon and chives; pulse until herbs are finely chopped. Makes about 2 cups; can be refrigerated up to 1 week.

3. To serve, arrange carrots over lettuce. Drizzle with dressing.

Homemade Tortilla Chips & Salsa
Servings: 2
Cooking Time: 8 Minutes

Ingredients:
- 6 corn tortillas (6-inch), cut into 6 pieces each
- Spray oil
- Salt, to taste
- Salsa, for serving

Directions:
1. Select the Preheat function on the Air Fryer, adjust the temperature to 330°F, then press Start/Pause.
2. Spray the tortilla chips with oil so they are evenly coated on both sides, then season lightly with salt.
3. Place the tortillas chips in the preheated air fryer basket.
4. Set the temperature to 330°F and the timer to 8 minutes, then press Start/Pause.
5. Shake the basket halfway through the cooking time.
6. Remove the chips when done, season with additional salt if desired, then serve with salsa.

Chestnut Stuffing
Servings: 5

Ingredients:
- 2 ounces onion, minced
- 2 ounces carrots, minced
- 2 ounces celery, minced
- 2 ounces white button mushrooms, minced

- 1½ tablespoons unsalted butter or bacon fat
- 12 ounces day-old bread, cubed
- 4 fluid ounces chicken stock, hot
- 1 egg, whisked
- 2 tablespoons parsley
- ½ teaspoon sage, chopped
- 6 ounces shelled, peeled, roasted chestnuts, quartered
- 1 teaspoon kosher salt
- ½ teaspoon ground black pepper
- 1 teaspoon ground nutmeg
- ¼ teaspoon ground ginger
- ¼ teaspoon ground mustard
- Gravy, for serving (optional)

Directions:
1. Sauté the onions, carrots, celery, and mushrooms in the butter (or bacon fat) until tender, about 5 minutes.
2. Combine the bread, chicken stock, egg, and sauteed vegetables in a large bowl.
3. Add the parsley, sage, chestnuts, salt, pepper, nutmeg, ginger, and mustard and mix until fully combined.
4. Select the Preheat function on the Air Fryer, set temperature to 330°F, and press Start/Pause.
5. Line the preheated air fryer basket with foil, being careful not to touch the hot surfaces.
6. Transfer the stuffing into the lined air fryer basket.
7. Select the Bake function, adjust temperature to 330°F and time to 30 minutes, press Shake, then press Start/Pause.
8. Cover the top of the stuffing with foil halfway through cooking. The Shake Reminder will let you know when.
9. Let the stuffing cool for 5 minutes inside the air fryer basket, then transfer to a serving dish.
10. Scoop the stuffing out into a dish or flip the stuffing out onto a cutting board and cut into individual servings.
11. Serve alongside your Thanksgiving dinner with gravy, if desired

SANDWICHES & BURGERS RECIPES

Beyond Burger In The Air Fryer
Servings: 4
Cooking Time: 10 Minutes

Ingredients:
- 2-4 Beyond Burger Patties
- 2 tsp of Weber Steak 'N Chop Seasoning

Directions:
1. Preheat your air fryer to 350 degrees and season your patties with ¼ tsp of seasoning on each side of the burger.
2. Place your burgers in the air fryer.
3. Cook at 350 for 9-11 minutes till the internal temperature is 165 degrees. Flip it half way through the cooking time.
4. Serve and enjoy!
NOTES
HOW TO REHEAT BEYOND BURGERS:
Add Beyond burger patties to the air fryer basket.
Air fry at 380 degrees for 3-4 minutes or until hot.

Air Fryer Hamburgers
Servings: 4
Cooking Time: 10 Minutes

Ingredients:
- 1 pound 90% lean ground beef
- 1 tablespoon extra-virgin olive oil
- 2 teaspoons Dijon mustard optional
- 1/2 teaspoon garlic powder
- 1/2 teaspoon kosher salt
- 1/2 teaspoon ground black pepper
- For Serving
- 4 hamburger buns we like brioche or pretzel buns, split, toasted if desired
- Toppings of choice: lettuce, sliced tomato, avocado, Barbecue Sauce, ketchup, etc.

Directions:
1. Place the beef in a large mixing bowl. Add the oil, mustard, garlic powder, salt, and pepper.

2. With a fork, gently stir to combine, being careful not to compact the meat (handle it as little as possible for the most tender burgers). Gently shape it into 4 equal patties that are 1/2-inch thick. With your thumb, gently press an indentation in the center.
3. Preheat the air fryer to 375 degrees F. Place the patties in the basket, leaving some space around each (cook in batches if needed). Air fry the burgers for 6 minutes, then flip and continue cooking until the internal temperature of the burger reaches 155 degrees F, about 2 to 4 minutes more. DO NOT overcook, or the burgers will be dry. If you'll be adding cheese, do so during the last minute of cooking. Serve hot on buns with your favorite toppings.
Notes
TO STORE: Store leftover burger patties in an airtight container for up to 3 days in the refrigerator.
TO REHEAT: Warm patties in a skillet, covered, with a bit of water to keep them from drying out.
TO FREEZE: Cooked burger patties can be frozen for up to 3 months in a freezer-safe container. Let thaw overnight in the refrigerator prior to reheating.

Air Fryer Falafel With Vegan Yogurt Tahini Sauce
Servings: 18
Cooking Time: 10 Minutes

Ingredients:
- For the Falafel
- 1 15 oz can chickpeas drained
- 1 cup chopped white onion
- 6 small cloves garlic
- 1 tablespoon lemon juice
- 1 cup lightly packed parsley leaves
- ½ cup lightly packed cilantro leaves
- ¼ cup lightly packed fresh dill leaves
- 1 teaspoon baking powder
- 2 teaspoons cumin

- 1 teaspoon salt
- ½ cup flour (either all-purpose flour or 1:1 gluten free flour)
- For the Vegan Yogurt Tahini Sauce
- 1 cup vegan plain yogurt (not vanilla flavored)
- 1 tablespoons tahini (see notes)
- 2 tablespoons lemon juice

Directions:
1. Add chickpeas, onion, garlic, lemon juice, parsley, cilantro, dill, flour, baking powder, cumin, and salt to a food processor. Pulse until a coarse crumb texture is formed. Stop to scrape down the sides of the bowl as needed.
2. Transfer the falafel mixture to a bowl, cover, and refrigerate for 1 hour (or up to 2 days before cooking).
3. While the falafel mixture sets, prepare the vegan tahini sauce. Whisk together the vegan yogurt, tahini, and lemon juice until combined. Add salt and pepper and stir to combine. Cover and refrigerate until time to serve.
4. Once the falafel mixture is chilled, use a spoon or cookie dough scooper to measure out 1 tablespoon of the dough. Form into balls. Place falafel balls on a plate. Repeat until all the batter has been used.
5. Spray the air fryer basket with vegetable cooking spray. Preheat air fryer to 375°F.
6. Use tongs to place raw falafel in the basket, arranging them on the bottom of the basket. Return basket to air fryer and cook for 15 minutes, removing the basket and using tongs to turn falafel once or twice during cooking time. Once done, remove falafel from the air fryer basket. Allow them to cool slightly.
7. To serve, place falafel on a plate and serve with tahini sauce for dipping. Or add 3–4 falafel inside a halved, pita along with hummus, chopped romaine lettuce, and chopped onions. Drizzle with the tahini sauce. Notes
Tahini is ground sesame seeds. If you don't have this, you can substitute almond butter or Sun Butter (made from ground sunflower seeds).

Air-fryer Chicken Katsu Sandwiches
Servings: 4

Ingredients:
- 2 8 ounce skinless, boneless chicken breast halves, halved crosswise
- ¼ cup reduced-sodium soy sauce
- 1 tablespoon toasted sesame oil, plus more for serving
- 1 tablespoon mirin (optional)
- 2 garlic cloves, minced
- ¼ cup all-purpose flour
- 1 teaspoon kosher salt
- ⅛ teaspoon black pepper
- 1 egg, lightly beaten
- 2 tablespoon mayonnaise or sour cream
- 1 teaspoon honey mustard or hot mustard (optional)
- 1 cup panko
- 1 - 2 tablespoon black and/or white sesame seeds
- Olive oil cooking spray
- 8 slices milk bread or 4 hamburger buns, split
- Desired toppers, such as shredded cabbage, bottled tonkatsu sauce*, chopped green onion, and/or mayonnaise (optional)

Directions:
1. Using the flat side of a meat mallet, lightly flatten chicken pieces between two pieces of plastic wrap to an even thickness. In a bowl or resealable bag combine soy sauce, the 1 Tbsp. sesame oil, mirin (if using), and garlic. Add chicken; turn to coat. Cover or seal, and chill 30 to 90 minutes.
2. In a shallow dish stir together flour, 1 tsp. kosher salt, and 1/8 tsp. ground black pepper. In a shallow bowl whisk together egg, mayonnaise, and mustard (if using). In another shallow dish combine panko and sesame seeds.
3. Remove chicken pieces from marinade; discard marinade. Coat chicken pieces with flour mixture, then dip in egg mixture. Coat with panko mixture, pressing to adhere. Coat one side of chicken pieces with olive oil nonstick cooking spray.

4. Preheat air fryer to 400°F.** Add chicken to basket, oil spray side up, and cook 4 minutes. Turn chicken, coat with additional olive oil cooking spray, and cook 4 to 5 minutes more or until golden brown and chicken reaches 165°F.

5. Serve chicken between slices of bread or on buns with desired toppers. If you like, drizzle with additional sesame oil to serve. Makes 4 sandwiches.

6. If you can't find bottled tonkatsu sauce, a sweet and savory Japanese condiment usually served with pork, you can make your own: In a small saucepan combine 1/2 cup ketchup, 2 Tbsp. soy sauce, 1 Tbsp. packed brown sugar, 1 Tbsp. mirin or rice vinegar, 1 1/2 tsp. Worcestershire sauce, 1 tsp. grated fresh ginger, and 2 cloves minced garlic. Heat over medium, stirring to dissolve sugar. Let cool. Refrigerate up to 1 week. Makes 3/4 cup.

7. Sheet Pan Variation

8. If you don't have an air fryer, preheat oven to 450°F. Place a wire rack in a sheet pan. Prepare chicken as directed through Step 3. Place chicken pieces on rack in prepared pan. Bake 15 minutes or until golden brown and chicken reaches 165°F. Serve as directed.

Air Fryer Mozzarella Mushroom Burgers

Servings: 4
Cooking Time: 25 Minutes

Ingredients:
- 8 portobello mushrooms (400g)
- 1 tablespoon balsamic vinegar
- 1 tablespoon extra virgin olive oil
- 4 large brioche buns (400g), split
- ¼ cup (75g) aioli
- 40 grams mixed salad leaves
- 1 large tomato (220g), sliced thinly
- 125 grams fresh mozzarella ball, cut into 4 slices
- 1/3 cup (90g) basil pesto
- to serve: shoestring fries and low-sugar tomato sauce

Directions:

1. Place mushrooms, vinegar and oil in a medium bowl; toss to coat. Season.

2. Preheat a 7-litre air fryer to 180°C/350°F for 3 minutes.

3. Taking care, place mushrooms in air fryer basket; at 180°C/350°F, cook for 12 minutes, turning halfway through cooking time, until tender.

4. Spread bun bases with aioli, then top with salad leaves, tomato, mozzarella, mushrooms and pesto; sandwich together with bun tops.

5. Serve mushroom burgers with shoestring fries and tomato sauce.

6 Ingredient Veggie Burgers

Servings: 6
Cooking Time: 10 Minutes

Ingredients:
- 1 tin black beans, drained and rinsed
- 1 onion finely chopped
- 2 garlic cloves, grated
- 1/3 cup roasted walnuts, roughly chopped
- 1/3 cup Oat flour*
- 1 Aubergine cut into bite-sized chunks
- Oat flour? Oat flour is simply porridge oats, popped into a blender, and ground until a fine powder. If you do not have oats, substitute this quantity for ¼ cup of wheat flour.

Directions:

1. Place the rinsed black beans into the basket of the Instant Pot Vortex, and air-fry on 205C for 5 minutes, until bursting and blistered.

2. While the beans cook, sprinkle ½ tsp of salt evenly over your aubergine and place it in a colander, to allow any bitter juices to drain out. Add the chopped onion to a frying pan with a little oil and cook until soft and translucent on a medium heat (about 4 minutes).

3. Once the beans have finished cooking, remove them from the basket and pop them into the bowl of a food processor.

4. Toss the aubergines in a little oil, then air fry them at 205C for 7 minutes, until golden and soft.

5. To the beans, add the grated garlic, cooked onions, walnuts, oat flour, and cooked aubergine. Pulse the mixture until the mixture comes together and starts forming a chunky paste. Then divide the mixture into 5 balls and shape them into patties.

6. Set the patties aside for 10 minutes to firm up. This is an important step, as the oat flour will absorb excess moisture in the patties, making them easier to cook and handle.

7. Set the Vortex air fryer to 190C. Brush the patties in olive oil, then place them into the air fryer for 6-9 minutes, until crisped and brown to your desired level.

8. Serve your veggie burgers with your favorite toppings on a soft roll (we love rocket, vegan aioli, and tomato) or omit the bun, and add your toppings to the patty, before wrapping it in butter lettuce, for a low carb alternative.

Air Fryer Frozen Impossible™ Burgers

Servings: 4
Cooking Time: 15 Minutes

Ingredients:
- 4 frozen Impossible™ Burger patties , 1/4lb (113g) patties
- salt , to taste
- black pepper , to taste
- oil spray , for coating
- BURGER ASSEMBLY:
- 4 Buns
- Optional - cheese, pickles, lettuce, onion, tomato, avocado, cooked bacon etc.
- EQUIPMENT
- Air Fryer
- Instant Read Thermometer (optional)

Directions:
1. Spray or brush both sides of the frozen patties with oil and season with salt and pepper.
2. Spray air fryer basket or rack with oil. Place the frozen patties in the air fryer basket/tray in a single layer. Air Fry at 380°F/193°C for 8 minutes.

3. Flip the patties and continue cooking for about 3-6 minutes or until cooked through and internal temperature is 160°F/71°C. Timing will vary depending on thickness of patties and individual air fryer model.
4. For Cheeseburgers: add the slices of cheese on top of the cooked patties. Air fry at 380°F/193°C for about 30 seconds to 1 minute to melt the cheese.
5. Warm the buns in the air fryer at 380°F/193°C for about 1 minute.
6. Serve on buns, topped with your favorite burger toppings.

Frozen Burgers In The Air Fryer

Servings: 2
Cooking Time: 10 Minutes

Ingredients:
- 2 frozen burger patties
- 2 slices cheddar cheese
- salt and pepper to taste
- toppings as desired

Directions:
1. Preheat your air fryer to 375°F.
2. Place the frozen burgers in the air fryer basket and cook for 5 minutes.
3. Flip the patties and cook for an additional 5 minutes. Add cheese in the last minute of cooking.
4. Top as desired and serve.
Notes
Avoid overcrowding the air fryer so the burger can cook evenly!

Homestyle Cheeseburgers

Servings: 4
Cooking Time: 15 Minutes

Ingredients:
- 1 pound ground beef chuck
- 1 ½ teaspoon kosher salt
- 1 teaspoon freshly ground black pepper
- 4 slices American cheese
- 4 sesame seed buns
- Ketchup, for serving
- 4 sesame seed buns

- Ketchup, for serving
- Yellow mustard, for serving
- Pickles, for serving

Directions:
1. Select Preheat on the Air Fryer, adjust the temperature to 400°F, then press Start/Pause.
2. Form the ground beef into 4 equally sized patties, a little less than ¾-inch thick. Season with the salt and pepper.
3. Place the beef patties into the preheated air fryer basket.
4. Set the temperature to 400°F and time to 14 minutes, then press Start/Pause.
5. Flip the burger patties over halfway through cooking.
6. Open the basket and top each patty with a slice of American cheese.
7. Set the temperature to 400°F and time to 1 minute, then press Start/Pause.
8. Remove the burger patties when done.
9. Place each patty on a sesame seed bun, dress the burgers with the condiments and pickles, then serve.

Air Fryer Burgers
Servings: 4
Cooking Time: 8 Minutes

Ingredients:
- 1 lb ground beef
- ¼ cup seasoned bread crumbs
- 2 tablespoons barbecue sauce
- 1 egg
- ¾ teaspoon seasoning salt
- ¼ teaspoon onion powder
- ¼ teaspoon garlic powder

Directions:
1. Preheat air fryer to 375 degrees F.
2. In a large bowl, combine beef, bread crumbs, barbecue sauce, egg, seasoning salt, onion powder and garlic powder.
3. Divide beef mixture into 4 sections and shape into patties (keep in mind they will shrink, so try to make them on the larger side).

4. Add patties to air fryer basket (you may have to work in batches depending on the size of your air fryer) and cook for 4-5 minutes per side (you don't have to flip, but they will brown evenly on both sides if you do), until an internal temperature of 160 degrees F is reached.
5. Serve on buns and with desired toppings.

Air Fryer Grilled Cheese Sandwiches
Servings: 2
Cooking Time: 8 Minutes

Ingredients:
- 2 tablespoons mayonnaise
- 4 thick slices country or sourdough bread
- 3 slices bacon halved crosswise
- 1 cup shredded Mexican blend or cheddar cheese

Directions:
1. Spread the mayonnaise on one side of each of the slices of bread. Place two slices of bread in the air fryer basket, mayo side facing down. Divide the shredded cheese over the tops of the two slices of bread. Cover the cheese with the remaining slices of bread, mayo side up.
2. Set the air fryer to 350°F for 6 to 8 minutes, or until the cheese is melted and the bread is crispy – it may not brown all that much. Cut in half and serve hot.
Notes
Other possible add-ins are:
Prosciutto
James, jellies and preserves
Pesto
Caramelized onions or shallots
Pickled Things (try sliced or chopped pickled brussels sprouts!)
Sliced Roasted Turkey Breast or Roast Chicken
Green Olive Tapenade
Roasted Peppers

SNACKS & APPETIZERS RECIPES

Garlic Parmesan Fries
Servings: 4

Ingredients:
- 2 russet potatoes
- 2 tablespoons olive oil
- ½ teaspoon seasoned salt or to taste
- 2 tablespoons butter
- 2 cloves garlic minced
- 2 tablespoons parmesan grated
- 1 tablespoon fresh parsley

Directions:
1. Scrub potatoes and cut into ¼" fries. Place in a large bowl of cold water and soak 30-60 minutes. Drain well and dab dry with a kitchen towel.
2. Preheat the air fryer to 390°F (or bake in the oven per directions in the notes).
3. Toss potatoes with oil and seasoned salt to taste and place in the air fryer basket.
4. Cook 10 minutes, shake/flip and cook an additional 6-8 minutes or until crisp.
5. While potatoes are cooking, place butter and garlic in a small dish and melt in the microwave until heated.
6. Once potatoes are crisp, remove them from the air fryer and place in a large bowl. Add garlic butter and toss well to combine. Add parmesan and parsley and toss.
7. Serve immediately.

Notes
Thicker fries may need more time, thinner fries may need a bit less time. Appliances can vary but it is easy to check on the fries a couple of minutes early and add more time if needed. To make more fries in the air fryer, cook several smaller batches. Once ready to serve, add all fries to the air fryer basket and cook at 390°F for 2-3 minutes or until heated through. Crisp up leftover air fryer French fries by placing them back into a preheated air fryer for about 3-5 minutes.
To bake in the oven, preheat the oven to 375°F. Spread drained and seasoned potatoes on a pan and bake for 20 minutes. Turn the oven up to 425° and cook fries until golden, about 20-25 minutes more.

Avocado Fries
Servings: 35
Cooking Time: 20 Minutes

Ingredients:
- 2 large avocados
- ½ cup unsweetened almond milk , may also sub with 1 large egg if not vegan
- ½ cup superfine blanched almond flour
- For the coating:
- 1 cup unsweetened toasted shredded coconut , OR sub with crushed Simple Mills Grain-Free Sea Salt Almond Flour Crackers (or other favorite grain-free crackers like Hu's Kitchen Grain-Free Crackers)
- 1.5 tbsp Cajun seasoning spice mix OR smoked paprika
- Salt and pepper
- For the optional dip:
- ⅓ cup vegan mayo
- 1 tbsp lemon juice
- ½ tbsp Cajun seasoning
- Salt and pepper to taste

Directions:
1. Use a large knife to cut your avocados in half and remove the pit from the middle. Cut the avocado into wedges or "fries".
2. Oven Directions:
3. Preheat oven to 400F. Line a large baking sheet with parchment paper.
4. Gather three wide shallow bowls. Place the almond milk in one bowl, the almond flour in the next bowl and combine the coating ingredients in the the third bowl.
5. Take one avocado slice, place it in the flour. Make sure it is fully coated in flour then gently shake to get rid of any excess flour.
6. Place it in the almond milk and again make sure it is fully coated and wet. You will find it easier if you use one hand for the first

two steps and then the other hand for the breading, so you don't get too messy!

7. Finally place it in the coconut breading, making sure it is fully coated, then place on the baking pan.

8. Repeat until all the slices are coated. Place the baking sheet in the oven for 15-20 minutes until turning golden brown.

9. FOR THE DIP:

10. Make the dip by mixing all the ingredients together. Enjoy with the avocado fries!

11. Air Fryer Directions:

12. Place the breaded avocado sticks in a single layer in the air fryer basket, you will have to work in batches.

13. Lightly coat with cooking spray and cook for 8-12 minutes at 375F, or until golden and crispy, flipping halfway through.

Air Fryer Waffle Fries

Servings: 4
Cooking Time: 10 Minutes

Ingredients:
- 1 pound frozen waffle fries
- ½ teaspoon seasoned salt (optional)

Directions:
1. Preheat Air Fryer to 400°F.
2. Add the waffle fries to the air fryer basket, filling about ½ full.
3. Cook for 10-12 minutes, shaking the basket after 5 minutes to prevent sticking.
4. Toss waffle fries with seasoned salt (if desired) and serve immediately.
Notes
To prevent the waffle fries from sticking to each other, lightly spray with pan release or a high smoke point cooking oil before cooking.

Air Fried Mummy Poppers

Ingredients:
- 10 jalapeño peppers
- 8 oz. softened cream cheese
- ½ teaspoon minced garlic
- 8 oz. pepper jack cheese
- 1 tsp of salt

- 1 scallion
- Candy Eyeballs
- Pillsbury Crescent Rolls
- 2 eggs

Directions:
1. Slice jalapeños in half and remove seeds.
2. Mince 1 green onion.
3. Slice or shred pepper jack cheese.
4. In a bowl, mix the cream cheese, salt, green onion, and pepper jack cheese.
5. In a separate bowl, whisk two eggs.
6. Unwrap 1 roll of Pillsbury crescent rolls.
7. Ignore perforations and cut into strips (we used a knife, but a pizza cutter would work great as well)
8. Fill each sliced pepper with cream cheese filling.
9. Wrap each stuffed pepper with strips of dough.
10. Place parchment round in Air Fryer basket.
11. Coat each pepper in egg before cooking.
12. Place jalapenos in air fryer (4 or 5 at a time, if you have the accessory pack try using the insert rack to cook more at a time)
13. Cook at 400F for 6 minutes
14. Decorate with candy eyes
15. Enjoy!

Sweet Potato Wedges

Servings: 4
Cooking Time: 12 Minutes

Ingredients:
- 2 small sweet potatoes cut into wedges (peeling optional)
- 2 tablespoons olive oil
- ¼ teaspoon salt and pepper each
- ¼ teaspoon smoked paprika
- ¼ teaspoon cumin

Directions:
1. Preheat the air fryer to 400°F.
2. Cut sweet potatoes into wedges and soak in cold water for 15-30 minutes.
3. When done soaking pat dry with paper towel and toss with olive oil and seasonings.
4. Place in the air fryer basket and cook for 11-12 minutes or until cooked.

Notes
Cut sweet potatoes to the same thickness to ensure they cook at the same rate.
Soaking sweet potatoes in cold water removes the starch and it is critical to getting that crispy exterior.

Dirty Katsu Halloumi Fries
Servings: 4
Cooking Time: 30 Minutes

Ingredients:
- 4 Potatoes
- 200g Grilling cheese or halloumi
- 200ml Chinese style curry cooking sauce
- 3 Spring onions, chopped
- 2 Small red onions, finely sliced
- 1 Handful coriander, finely chopped
- 1 Teaspoon chilli flakes
- Hot sauce (optional)
- Any plain cereal for breadcrumbs: cornflakes/rice krispies/oats

Directions:
1. Slice up the halloumi into thin slices. Crack an egg into a bowl and whisk. Place whatever cereal you're using for your breadcrumbs into a blender and blitz until fine.
2. Chop up your potatoes into chips, place them in a bowl, drizzle with oil and add 1 teaspoon of smoked paprika, 1 teaspoon garlic powder and plenty of salt and pepper.
3. Place them in the air fryer for 12 minutes on 200 degrees or in the oven for 30/40 minutes on a baking tray. Chips should be golden all over.
4. Finely slice your onion and fry these in oil until super crispy and golden.
5. Whilst they're both cooking, dip halloumi slices in egg then into your blended cereal and set aside ready to air fry. (You can also shallow fry these with oil in another pan too if you don't have a double tray air fryer or don't want to wait for chips to finish cooking).
6. Air fry your halloumi for 8 minutes on 200 degrees or shallow fry in oil for 10 minutes.
7. Add Chinese cooking sauce to a jug and heat up in microwave.
8. Finely chop your fresh coriander and spring onions.
9. When chips are cooked, add them to bowls. Drizzle with curry sauce, place halloumi and crispy onions on top. Layer coriander and spring onions over and drizzle hot sauce over everything.

Crispy Air Fryer Potato Skins

Ingredients:
- Potato skins
- Olive oil
- Salt
- Pepper
- Potato spice

Directions:
1. In a bowl, drizzle potato skins with olive oil, salt, pepper, potato spice and mix. Place the potato skins in the air fryer at 180 degrees for 10 minutes, time will also depend on how crispy you like your potato skins and enjoy!

Air Fryer Green Beans
Servings: 4
Cooking Time: 10 Minutes

Ingredients:
- 1 pound Green Beans
- 1 tbsp olive oil
- 1 tsp salt
- 1/2 tsp black pepper

Directions:
1. Trim the ends of the green beans, then rinse in water.
2. In a large bowl combine the beans with olive oil, salt and optional black pepper. Toss the ingredients together until they beans are coated.
3. Next, transfer them to the air fryer basket, and then lay them in a single layer. Work in batches if necessary. (One pound green beans is usually two batches.)
4. Cook at 400 degrees F for 8-10 minutes, tossing one or two times during cooking, until they reach the desired crispness you prefer.

5. Remove the beans with tongs, and add additional salt, parmesan cheese, or your favorite extra seasonings.

NOTES

Depending on your air fryer, cooking times may vary. Add 1-2 minutes if necessary.

Air Fryer Chickpeas

Servings: 1
Cooking Time: 15 Minutes

Ingredients:

- 1 x 400g tin chickpeas, drained and rinsed
- 1 tbsp olive oil
- 2 tsp spice or herb seasoning*

Directions:

1. Drain and rinse the chickpeas.
2. Add the oil and your choice of spices or herbs (see notes).
3. Toss the chickpeas until they are coated in the oil and seasoning.
4. Transfer to the air fryer basket and set off at 200°C (190°F), and air fry for 15 minutes, shaking two or three times.
5. The chickpeas should be hard and crispy when they are ready. If they are still a little soft, air fry them for a few more minutes. Add extra seasoning if required.

Notes

*Seasoning

You can use any seasoning you like. Suggestions include;

Piri Piri
Smoked Paprika
Garlic Salt
Garlic and Herb
Mixed Herbs
Curry Powder

Green Bean Fries

Servings: 4
Cooking Time: 10 Minutes

Ingredients:

- ¾ pound fresh green beans washed and trimmed
- oil for frying
- kosher salt to taste

- Batter Ingredients
- 1 cup all-purpose flour
- 1 cup milk
- 1 egg
- 1 teaspoon baking powder
- 1 teaspoon paprika
- 1 teaspoon garlic powder, or dried dill optional
- 1 teaspoon each salt and pepper

Directions:

1. Heat a deep fryer or a shallow pan of oil to 375°F.
2. Trim the ends off the beans and ensure they are dry.
3. Combine all batter ingredients together in a medium bowl and whisk until smooth. Let rest 5 minutes.
4. Using a fork dip the beans into the batter, a couple at a time, coating them completely.
5. Place the beans into the deep fryer or oil in small batches for about 2-3 minutes or until browned and crispy. Don't overcrowd them.
6. Remove from oil, drain on paper towels, and sprinkle with seasoned salt.

Air Fryer Sweet Potato French Fries

Servings: 4
Cooking Time: 20 Minutes

Ingredients:

- 1 pound (454 g) sweet potatoes , cut into 1/4" french fry size
- 2 teaspoons (10 ml) olive oil
- salt , to taste
- 1/4 teaspoon (1.25 ml) garlic powder , optional
- ground black pepper , to taste

Directions:

1. We like to keep the skin-on for crispier fries. But you can peel the sweet potatoes if you want. Wash and dry the sweet potatoes completely. Cut the sweet potatoes into french fry size and thickness. Keep them same sized as possible for even cooking.
2. Transfer the sweet potatoes in a bowl and then lightly coat them with olive oil. Sprinkle

salt and pepper (and/or garlic powder) evenly over the sweet potatoes. Genlty toss to evenly coat all the fries with oil and seasonings.

3. Lay the sweet potatoes in the air fryer basket and spread them into an even layer.

4. Air Fry at 380°F for about 18-22 minutes. A couple times during cooking, gently shake the basket, turn or toss the sweet potatoes to help them cook evenly. Try not to break them. For crisper potatoes, shake them again and cook for an additional 2-4 minutes or until they are your desired texture and doneness.

NOTES

Recipes were cooked in 3-4 qt air fryers. If using a larger air fryer, the recipe might cook quicker so adjust cooking time.

Remember to set a timer to shake/flip/toss the food as directed in recipe.

Fries

Servings: 4
Cooking Time: 8 Minutes

Ingredients:

- 6 Potatoes, sliced into chips
- Olive oil, to toss
- Chilli seasoning, to season
- Salt, to season

Directions:

1. Rinse and dry the chips well, toss in olive oil, chilli and salt.

2. Spray the basket with olive oil spray and layer the chips (if using Duo Crisp) or lie flat across the Vortex drawer.

3. Bake at 200C for 5-8 minutes, turning / tossing halfway when prompted.

Chunky Chips

Servings: 2
Cooking Time: 30 Minutes

Ingredients:

- 2 medium potatoes approx. 425g/15oz total
- low calorie cooking spray
- 2 pinches garlic salt
- 1 pinch salt

Directions:

1. Preheat the oven to 200-210°C.

2. Peel the potatoes and cut them into chunky chips (the chunkier the better).

3. Place the potatoes in a pan and cover with boiling water, add a good pinch of salt.

4. Bring back up to the boil and let it boil for 2 minutes.

5. Drain the potatoes and place them in a large bowl.

6. Spray generously with low calorie cooking spray and add a good pinch of garlic salt. Toss them in the bowl to make sure they are evenly coated, then repeat (spray, sprinkle and toss).

7. Spray an oven tray with low calorie cooking spray then tip on the potatoes and spread them out evenly.

8. Cook in oven for around 30 minutes. Halfway through cooking, flip the chips over so they colour evenly.

Air Fryer Cream Cheese Wontons

Servings: 4
Cooking Time: 10 Minutes

Ingredients:

- 8 ounce cream cheese softened
- 2 Tablespoons green onion finely chopped
- 1/2 teaspoon garlic powder
- 1/4 teaspoon salt
- wonton wrappers
- olive oil spray

Directions:

1. In a small bowl add the cream cheese, green onions, garlic powder and salt and beat until creamy.

2. Lay a wonton wrapper on a non stick surface. With your finger wet the edges of the wonton wrapper. Add about a teaspoon of the cream cheese filling and bring up each corner creating a star and seal tightly.

3. Spray the basket of an air fryer with olive oil spray. Add the wontons to the basket and lightly spray with olive oil. Cook at 370 degrees for 8 minutes. Check to see if they are golden and cook for an additional 2 minutes if needed.

Air Fryer Kale Chips

Servings: 4
Cooking Time: 3 Minutes

Ingredients:
- 1 bunch kale
- 2 teaspoons olive oil
- 1/2 teaspoon salt

Directions:
1. Wash the kale and pat dry until completely dry. Roughly tear the leaves into bite sized pieces.
2. Add the kale to a mixing bowl, then drizzle with olive oil. Using your hands, rub the leaves to ensure they have some oil on them. Sprinkle the salt all over.
3. Transfer the kale to the air fryer basket and air fry at 190C/375F for 3-4 minutes, ensuring they don't burn.
4. Repeat the process until all the kale chips are cooked.
Notes
TO STORE: It's best to store the cooled kale chips in a paper bag at room temperature to prevent them from becoming soggy. They should stay crisp for up to 3 days.

Air Fryer Everything Bagel Avocado Fries

Servings: 4

Ingredients:
- 1/4 c. all-purpose flour
- 2 large eggs
- 3/4 c. panko breadcrumbs
- 3 tbsp. everything bagel seasoning
- 2 tbsp. black and/or white sesame seeds
- 2 large, just ripe avocados, halved, pitted, peeled, and sliced ½" thick
- Olive oil cooking spray
- 2 oz. cream cheese
- 1 tbsp. (or more) water
- lime wedges, for serving

Directions:
1. Pour flour into a shallow bowl. In another shallow bowl, beat eggs to blend. In a third shallow bowl, mix panko, everything bagel seasoning, and sesame seeds. Dip avocado strips into flour, shaking off any excess. Dip into eggs, then into panko mixture, gently pressing to adhere. Transfer to a plate.
2. Lightly coat an air-fryer basket with cooking spray. Working in batches, arrange avocado in a single layer in basket, spacing about 1/4" apart; spray with cooking spray. Cook at 350°, flipping halfway through and spraying with cooking spray, until golden and crisp, 6 to 8 minutes. Clean out any breading in basket between batches.
3. In a small heatproof bowl, microwave cream cheese on high until melted and smooth, about 30 seconds. Stir in water, adding more if necessary to create a drizzleable consistency.
4. Drizzle avocado fries with melted cream cheese. Serve with lime wedges alongside.

Tater Tots In The Air Fryer

Servings: 4
Cooking Time: 7 Minutes

Ingredients:
- 16 ounces frozen tater tots

Directions:
1. Preheat your air fryer to 400 degrees.
2. Place the frozen tater tots into the air fryer filling the basket no more than halfway.
3. Cook tater tots for 7 to 9 minutes, shaking the basket halfway through.
4. Remove tots from the air fryer and enjoy immediately with your favorite dipping sauce.

Baked Chipotle Sweet Potato Fries

Servings: 1
Cooking Time: 25 Minutes

Ingredients:
- 1 medium sweet potato ((about 6 ounces) peeled)
- 1 teaspoon olive oil
- 1/4 teaspoon kosher salt
- 1/4 teaspoon garlic powder
- 1/4 teaspoon ground chipotle chile powder

- olive oil spray

Directions:
1. Oven Directions:
2. Preheat oven to 425F.
3. In a medium bowl, toss sweet potatoes with olive oil, salt, garlic powder and chipotle chile powder.
4. Spread potatoes on a baking sheet. Avoid crowding so potatoes get crisp. Bake 15 minutes. Turn and bake an additional 10-15 minutes. Ovens may vary so keep an eye on them and be sure to cut all the potatoes the same size to ensure even cooking.
5. Air Fryer Directions:
6. Preheat air fryer to 400°F.
7. Slice the potato into even 1/4 inch thick fries. Toss with oil, salt, garlic powder, and chipotle chile powder.
8. Transfer to the air fryer basket, spritz the top with olive oil then cook 400F in a single layer without overcrowding the basket until golden brown and crisp on the outside, about 7 to 8 minutes, turning half way.

Yuca Fries Recipe
Servings: 6
Cooking Time: 30 Minutes

Ingredients:
- 1 large (900 g) yuca root (cassava)
- ½ tsp salt
- ½ tsp paprika
- ½ tsp garlic powder
- ½ tsp onion powder
- Black pepper to taste
- 2 tbsp oil

Directions:
1. Peel and slice it
2. You can watch the short video for visual instructions.
3. To peel the yuca root, start by cutting off both ends. If the root has a thin peel (like mine had), simply use a peeler. If not, then make a thin slice down the length of the root. You can then dig a finger underneath the peel and peel it away by hand.
4. Slice the yuca root into sticks: Cut it into 3 to 4-inch-long sections and then slice it into batons/wedges (refer to images/video in the post).
5. Boil it
6. Soak in cold water for about 5 minutes, then drain the water.
7. Boil the sticks in plenty of fresh salted water for about 20 minutes, or until fork-tender.
8. Drain the water very well (optionally pat-dry with a kitchen towel), then add the cooked yuca sticks to a large bowl together with all other ingredients.
9. Toss to combine until well coated.
10. Cook it (air fryer method)
11. Finally, transfer the fries to your air fryer basket in a single layer, with space in between (cook in batches if necessary). Depending on the thickness of the yuca fries, cook at 380 °F (190 °C) for about 15-18 minutes or, until golden brown and crispy.
12. Check the recipe notes below for the oven and skillet method.
13. Enjoy with a dip of choice like this yum yum sauce or vegan mayonnaise!

Notes

Skillet Directions:

Prepare the yuca root as written (minus seasoning the fries). Meanwhile, heat a large, wide skillet with at-least ½-1 inch of oil over medium-high heat.

Once hot (around 375F/190C), transfer the fries in batches and cook, flipping halfway, until golden-brown and crispy.

Use a slotted spoon to transfer the cooked cassava fries to paper towels to drain excess oil, then season and enjoy.

Oven Directions:

Follow the recipe, but instead of transferring them to an air fryer, spread them across a parchment paper-lined baking sheet.

Bake in a preheated oven at 425F/220C for about 25 minutes, turning halfway. Baked yuca fries won't be as crispy, but are delicious. Cooking time will vary: Based on how thick you cut the fries.

Air Fryer Pumpkin Seeds Recipe

Servings: 4
Cooking Time: 10-15 Minutes

Ingredients:

* 1 (10- to 15-pound) large pumpkin
* 1 teaspoon olive oil
* 1/4 teaspoon ground chipotle pepper
* 1/4 teaspoon kosher salt, plus more as needed
* 1/8 teaspoon cayenne pepper

Directions:

1. Cut the top off a large pumpkin and scoop out the seeds. Rinse in a colander under running water to separate from the pulp. Lay the seeds out on paper towels and pat dry. Let sit for 30 minutes to remove any excess moisture. You should have about 1 cup pumpkin seeds.
2. Heat the air fryer to 350°F. Transfer the dried pumpkin seeds to a medium bowl. Add 1 teaspoon olive oil, 1/4 teaspoon ground chipotle pepper, 1/4 teaspoon kosher salt, and 1/8 teaspoon cayenne pepper. Toss to combine.
3. Spread the seeds evenly in the basket of the air fryer. Cook, shaking the basket halfway through cooking, until the seeds are golden and crispy, 10 to 15 minutes total. Transfer to a bowl and let cool. Taste and season with more salt as needed.

RECIPE NOTES

Yield: If your pumpkin yields more than 1 cup seeds, adjust the oil and seasonings as necessary. If you are making a larger quantity of pumpkin seeds, they will likely need to be cooked in batches for even roasting.

How To Bake Sweet Potatoes

Cooking Time: 50 Minutes

Ingredients:

* Large sweet potatoes (however many you want)

Directions:

1. Preheat the oven to 425°F (218°C). Lightly slash or prick the sweet potatoes several times with a sharp knife to allow for even ventilation. This allows steam to escape and allows the heat to get into the insides of the potato, which in turn helps the potatoes bake evenly throughout and prevents them from bursting in the oven.
2. Place the potatoes on a baking sheet (I line mine with parchment paper for easy cleanup). Bake for 45-60 minutes, or until the potatoes are fork tender and don't give any resistance.*

Notes

Smaller sweet potatoes will need about 40-45 minutes. Really large sweet potatoes will need 60-70 minutes.

Air Fryer Carrot Fries

Servings: 2
Cooking Time: 8 Minutes

Ingredients:

* 3 medium carrots sliced into sticks
* 1 tablespoon olive oil
* ½ teaspoon salt
* ½ teaspoon pepper
* ¼ teaspoon garlic powder
* Dipping Sauce
* ¼ cup mayonnaise
* 1 tablespoon honey
* ½ teaspoon Sriracha

Directions:

1. Preheat air fryer to 400°F.
2. Slice carrots into fries and toss with oil and seasonings.
3. Place in a single layer in air fryer basket and cook for 5-6 minutes, shaking basket halfway through cooking.
4. Combine mayonnaise, honey, and sriracha in a small bowl and whisk till combined.

Notes

Leftover air fryer carrot fries can be kept in a covered container in the refrigerator for up to 3 days. Reheat fries in the air fryer and season before serving.

Keto Fried Pickles

Servings: 4
Cooking Time: 7 Minutes

Ingredients:
- 9 large pickles sliced lengthways
- 3/4 + 1 tablespoon almond flour
- 1/2 teaspoon salt
- 1/4 teaspoon pepper
- 1 cup parmesan cheese
- 2 large eggs
- 2 tablespoons sour cream

Directions:
1. Slice your dill pickles lengthways and set aside.
2. In a small bowl, add your almond flour, salt, pepper, and parmesan cheese and mix until combined. In a separate bowl, whisk together the eggs and sour cream.
3. Dip the dill pickles in the wet mixture, followed by the dry mixture. Repeat the process until all the pickles are battered.
4. Add some oil to a non-stick pan. Once hot, add the battered pickles to it and fry for 3-4 minutes, flipping halfway through, until golden brown.
5. Serve the fried pickles immediately with your favorite condiments.
Notes
If you'd like to make this in an air fryer, simply prepare as instructed. Once ready to cook, add them to an air fryer basket and air fry at 200C/400F for 8 minutes.
TO STORE: Leftover pickles should be stored in the refrigerator, covered, for up to three days.
TO FREEZE: Place the cooked and cooled pickles in an airtight container and store them in the freezer for up to two months.
REHEAT: As the fried pickles are 'battered', they should not be microwaved. Instead, reheat them in the air fryer or in a preheated oven.

Roasted Garlic Hummus

Ingredients:
- 1 bulb of garlic cloves, separated and unpeeled
- 5 tbsp olive oil, divided
- can of tinned chickpeas in water
- 2 tbsp light tahini
- sea salt
- 1 pinch of white pepper
- 1 tsp lemon juice
- 2 tbsp water
- fresh parsley to garnish

Directions:
1. Preheat air fryer oven to 350°F. Place the separated, unpeeled garlic cloves into a small oven-safe dish. Cover in 2 tbsp olive oil and roast for 20 minutes.
2. Remove the dish from the oven and leave to cool for 1 hour. While you wait, drain and rinse the chickpeas well and remove any skins they might have. Place the chickpeas into the blender. Squeeze the cooled roasted garlic into the blender, as well.
3. Then, add in the remaining olive oil, tahini, sea salt, white pepper, lemon juice and 1 tbsp of water. Blend until creamy. Add more water if needed and garnish with chopped parsley and an extra drizzle of olive oil. Serve with your desired crackers or chips.

Air-fried Chips

Servings: 4
Cooking Time: 35 Minutes

Ingredients:
- 4-5 large potatoes, about 1kg
- 1 tbsp sunflower or olive oil

Directions:
1. To make straight, neat chips, peel the potatoes and trim away all the rounded edges so they become rectangular blocks. Cut the blocks into batons – they should be somewhere between fries and thick chips, as if they're too thin, they might break; too thick, and they won't cook through (if you like, save the offcuts to make mash or add to soups).

Alternatively, cut the unpeeled potatoes into chips without trimming, if you're not bothered by neatness. Rinse the chips and pat dry with a clean tea towel.

2. Tip the chips into the bottom of an air fryer (the part with the paddle), add the oil, and toss the chips in the oil so they are evenly coated. Program the fryer to cook for 30 mins using the paddle. After this time, check that the chips are tender and cooked through. If they're not, cook for a further 5 mins. Season well.

Crispy Air Fryer Chickpeas

Servings: 3
Cooking Time: 15 Minutes

Ingredients:

• 15 ounce can chickpeas (rinsed and drained)
• Extra virgin olive oil spray
• 1 teaspoon dried spices of your choice (such as Cajun seasoning, garlic salt, blackened seasoning, montreal steak seasoning, zatar, etc)

Directions:

1. Drain chickpeas in a colander and transfer to a plate lined with paper towels.
2. Let them dry completely.
3. Transfer the chickpeas to the air fryer basket in a single layer and air fry 380F about 12 to 15 minutes, shaking the basket every 5 minutes until crunchy on the inside, not moist and golden brown on the outside.
4. Transfer the chickpeas to a medium bowl while still hot, spritz all over with olive oil and immediately toss with the spices. Eat at room temperature as a snack or over your favorite salad.

Notes

Tip for crunchy chickpeas: It's important to start with dry chickpeas or they won't get crisp and if they do, they won't stay crisp. Dry them well on paper towels, then if time permits leave them out an hour to hour dry before cooking.

Storage: Store chickpeas in a jar at room temperature up to a week. If leftover chickpeas get soft you can pop them back in the air fryer 2 to 3 minutes to crisp them back up.

Seasoning Ideas:

You can use whatever spices you want for these crispy chickpeas. They are a blank canvas, so get creative! Here are some ideas:

Cajun seasoning
Garlic salt
Blackened seasoning
Montreal steak seasoning
Za'atar
Tajin
Curry powder
Grated Parmesan cheese
Ranch seasoning (garlic and onion powders, salt, pepper, and dried parsley and dill)

FAVORITE AIR FRYER RECIPES

Pepperoni Pizza

Ingredients:
- 11 oz. Pre-made pizza dough
- 5 Tbsp. Pizza sauce
- 1 cup Mozzarella cheese
- 10-12 Pepperonis

Directions:
1. Use your hands to stretch the pre-made dough out into a shape that will fit in air fryer.
2. Spread sauce over dough, leaving a ¼-inch border. Sprinkle mozzarella cheese over sauce and place pepperonis on top.
3. Cook pizza at 400 degrees for 15 minutes, depending on desired level of crispiness.
4. Plate, serve, and enjoy!

Nana's Macaroni

Ingredients:
- 12 oz. tomato sauce
- 6 oz. Colby cheese, grated
- ¾ stick of butter, cut into chunks
- ¾ of a lb. macaroni elbows, cooked
- 1 cup milk
- salt and pepper to taste

Directions:
1. Cook your pasta and then grate your cheese. Put the cooked pasta and some of the cheese into your dish. Add in the tomato sauce, butter and milk. Sprinkle salt and pepper to taste. Or add "one cross" salt and pepper, according to Rachel's Nana. Then, add in the rest of the cheese, mixing thoroughly.
2. Cover your dish with tinfoil and place it in your Air Fryer Oven. Using the Manual mode, bake it at 350°F for 30 minutes. Once the timer goes off, give it good stir. If desired, replace the tinfoil and place the dish back in the Air Fryer Oven. Cook for an additional 5-10 minutes and enjoy!

Air Fryer Pizza Quesadilla
Servings: 2
Cooking Time: 8 Minutes

Ingredients:
- 2 flour tortillas 8-inch
- 1 cup mozzarella cheese shredded
- 10 slices pepperoni
- 2 tbsp pizza sauce
- ½ tsp Italian seasoning
- ½ tsp butter melted and unsalted
- ½ tsp Parmesan cheese

Directions:
1. Remove tortillas from packaging and brush one side of each tortilla with melted butter.
2. Place each tortilla in air fryer basket, brushed side down. 3. Spread a thin layer of pizza sauce, pepperoni slices, shredded cheese, and Italian seasoning on top of tortilla.
3. Fold each tortilla in half and gently press together or seal them with a toothpick.
4. Air fry at 350 degrees F for 8-10 minutes, flipping the tortilla halfway through cooking time, until you have a crispy tortilla that is golden brown. After two minutes of air frying, open basket and if tortillas have opened, gently press together. The melted cheese will now keep them sealed.
5. Remove tortillas and brush again with a light coat of butter then sprinkle with parmesan cheese before serving.
NOTES
I make this recipe in my Cosori 5.8 qt. air fryer or 6.8 quart air fryer. Depending on your air fryer, size and wattages, cooking time may need to be adjusted 1-2 minutes.
An easy way to store leftovers is to let them cool after cooking and then place quesadillas in an airtight container to save for later. Leftovers of this make for a quick dinner. You can also wrap leftovers in plastic wrap and store them in the fridge as well.

Air Fryer Pitta Pizza

Servings: 4

Ingredients:

- 4 gluten free pitta breads
- 4 tbsp (60ml) gluten free bbq sauce
- 80g grated cheddar cheese
- 80g diced mozzarella
- 60g diced cooked chicken
- 40g sliced mini pepperoni
- 40g diced red pepper
- Pinch chilli flakes
- COOKING MODE
- When entering cooking mode - We will enable your screen to stay 'always on' to avoid any unnecessary interruptions whilst you cook!

Directions:

1. Place the air fryer basket in your Foodi
2. Spread the bbq sauce over each pitta bread
3. Sprinkle on the cheddar and mozzarella
4. Top each pitta with the chicken, pepperoni, red pepper and chilli flakes
5. Cook the pittas one at a time in your Foodi on 180oc for 7 minutes
6. Repeat until all the pizzas are cooked
7. Serve with a side salad

Air-fryer Brats With Beer Gravy

Servings: 5

Ingredients:

- 1 package uncooked bratwurst links (20 ounces)
- 2 tablespoons butter
- 1 medium onion, thinly sliced
- 2 tablespoons all-purpose flour
- 1/8 teaspoon dill weed
- 1/8 teaspoon pepper
- 1 bottle (12 ounces) beer or nonalcoholic beer
- 5 slices thick bread

Directions:

1. Preheat air fryer to 400°. Place bratwurst in a single layer in a greased air fryer. Cook until no longer pink, 8-10 minutes.

2. Meanwhile, in a large saucepan, heat butter over medium-high heat. Add onion; cook and stir until onions start to brown and soften. Add flour, dill weed and pepper; stir until smooth. Stir in beer. Bring to a boil. Reduce heat; simmer, stirring constantly until thickened, 3-5 minutes. To serve, place 1 brat on each slice of bread; top evenly with onion mixture.

Air Fryer Brats

Servings: 5
Cooking Time: 13 Minutes

Ingredients:

- 1 pound uncooked bratwurst
- 5 hoagie rolls optional

Directions:

1. Preheat the air fryer to 360°F.
2. Place the brats in a single layer in the air fryer.
3. Cook for 8 minutes. Flip the brats over and cook an additional 5-7 minutes or until cooked through and the internal temperature reaches 165°F.
4. Serve in rolls with desired toppings.
Notes
Keep brats warm in a dish covered with foil in the oven until ready to serve.

Italian Sausage In Air Fryer

Servings: 4
Cooking Time: 22 Minutes

Ingredients:

- 1 medium red bell pepper
- 1 medium green bell pepper
- 1 small onion
- 4 Italian Sausage links
- 4 sausage rolls or hamburger buns

Directions:

1. Slice the bell peppers and onion into long strips and set aside.
2. Preheat the air fryer to 320 degrees Fahrenheit for 2-3 minutes.
3. Add peppers and onions into the basket of the air fryer and use the air fry function to

cook at 320 degrees Fahrenheit for 10-12 minutes, tossing halfway through the cooking process.

4. Remove peppers and onions from the air fryer basket and set them aside.

5. Increase the temperature of the air fryer to 370 degrees Fahrenheit and add Italian sausage links to the basket.

6. Air fry at 370 degrees F for 10-12 minutes, flipping the links halfway through the cooking process. 7. Remove the sausage links from the air fryer and set them aside.

7. Slice open the sausage rolls, place them into the basket, and carefully add the sausage links and top them with the cooked peppers and onions. 8. Cook at 370 degrees F for 1-2 minutes.

8. Serve.

NOTES

This recipe was made in a 5.8 qt Cosori Air Fryer so make sure to adjust your total cooking time depending on the size of your air fryer.

If you want to add the sausage to hot dog buns, you can easily make killer sausage, onion, and pepper sandwiches!

If you want to skip the carbs, skip the buns!

Add a bit of heat and spice to your serving only by sprinkling on some cayenne pepper to the mixture!

If you're a fan of dips, a tad bit of marinara sauce goes a long way!

Air Fryer Gnocchi, Sausage, And Green Beans

Servings: 4
Cooking Time: 10 Minutes

Ingredients:
*   1/2 pound green beans, washed, trimmed, and cut in half
*   4 Italian sausages
*   12 ounces gnocchi (frozen or refrigerated both work great)
*   1 teaspoon Italian seasoning
*   1 tablespoon extra-virgin olive oil
*   salt and pepper to taste

Directions:

1. Preheat your air fryer to 380 degrees.

2. Cut the Italian sausage into 1-inch slices and place aside.

3. Place green beans and gnocchi into a bowl and mix with extra-virgin olive oil, Italian seasoning, salt, and pepper.

4. Add sausage slices to the air fryer then place the green beans and gnocchi on top. Do not shake or stir!

5. Cook for 10-12 minutes until the Italian sausage reaches an internal temperature of 160 degrees, shaking the basket halfway through.

6. Remove from the air fryer and enjoy!

Air Fryer Churros Twists

Servings: 2
Cooking Time: 12 Minutes

Ingredients:
*   1 and 3/4 cups of The Pantry Self Raising Flour
*   100g of Everyday Essentials Milk Chocolate
*   1 cup of Brooklea Greek Style Natural Yogurt
*   2 tablespoons of Sugar
*   1 tablespoon of Ground Cinnamon

Directions:
1. Makes 6 large or 12 small churros.

2. Add 1 and 3/4 of a cup of self raising flour to a bowl with 1 cup of Greek yoghurt.

3. Mix together with your hands. If the mixture is sticking to your hands after all flour has been mixed in, add more flour, tablespoons at a time.

4. Place some more flour on your kitchen surface and roll mixture into a large sausage shape. Divide this into either 6 or 12.

5. Roll your smaller pieces into long sausage shapes and bend them in half at the middle. Plait each side over each other to create a twist.

6. Brush with plenty of oil and place in the airfryer for 12 minutes on 200 degrees until golden brown.

7. Meanwhile, on a plate put 2 tablespoons of sugar and 1 tablespoon of ground cinnamon and mix together.

8. Remove churros and place in the sugar, ensuring all sides are coated.

9. Melt chocolate in the microwave and serve with churros.

Air Fried Cauliflower Pizza Crust

Ingredients:
- For crust:
- 1 head of cauliflower
- ½ cup of shredded mozzarella
- ¼ cup grated Parmesan
- ½ teaspoon dried oregano
- ½ teaspoon kosher salt
- ¼ teaspoon garlic powder
- 2 eggs, lightly beaten
- For toppings:
- Pizza sauce
- Pepperoni
- Mushrooms
- Mozzarella

Directions:
1. Break cauliflower in florets and pulse in food processor until fine.
2. Steam cauliflower in a steamer basket and drain well. We used a paper towel to help speed up the process.
3. In a bowl, combine the mozzarella, Parmesan, oregano, salt, garlic powder, and eggs. Once the cauliflower is ready add that to the same bowl. We used a spatula.
4. Transfer to parchment paper and shape into pizza, whatever size you'd like.
5. Place the pizza in the air fryer. Set the air fryer at 350 F for 14 minutes.
6. The pizza crust is done, but we went a step further and made some pepperoni and mushroom pizza.
7. To add the pizza sauce, flip over the crust and spread the sauce evenly.
8. Add mozzarella, or whichever cheese you'd like, then add pepperoni and mushrooms (or your favorite toppings).
9. Place back in air fryer and set the time for 4 minutes at 350 F. For different toppings, time may vary from 2-4 minutes.
10. Take out your cauliflower pizza and enjoy!

Air Fryer Pizza
Servings: 2
Cooking Time: 10 Minutes

Ingredients:
- 1 pkg pizza dough mix 6.5 oz. , used Betty Crocker mix with water
- 1/4 c spaghetti sauce
- 1/2-3/4 c mozzarella cheese
- pepperoni optional
- olives optional
- olive oil spray

Directions:
1. Preheat your air fryer at 320 degrees for 3 minutes.
2. Make your pizza dough. Spray 7" springform pan and spread dough inside so it is level across the pan.
3. Put into air fryer and spray top of raw pizza dough with olive oil.
4. Close lid/drawer and set to 320 degrees for 3 minutes so dough can cook a bit.
5. Open and add pizza sauce, cheese, pepperoni and other toppings.
6. Close lid/drawer again and reset to 320 degrees for 7 minutes. Add 1 more minute if you want top crispier. Enjoy!

Air Fryer Sausage Stuffing
Servings: 4
Cooking Time: 15 Minutes

Ingredients:
- 6 oz. (170 g) box stuffing mix (not 12 oz.)
- 4 Tablespoons (60 g) butter
- 1/2 onion , diced
- 2 stalks celery , diced
- 1/2 lb. (227 g) raw sausage
- 1/2 teaspoon (2.5 ml) garlic powder , or to taste
- 1 1/2 cups (360 ml) chicken or beef broth or water
- 1-2 Tablespoons (15-30 ml) chopped fresh or dried herbs (parsley, sage, rosemary, etc) , optional
- Black pepper , to taste
- Salt , to taste if needed

- 2 Tablespoons (30 g) additional melted butter , for brushing
- OPTIONAL ADDITIONAL STUFFING EXTRAS:
- chopped bacon, chopped nuts, dried fruit, mushrooms, etc.
- EQUIPMENT
- Air Fryer
- 7" Accessory Cake Bucket Pan
- Aluminum Foil
- Oil Sprayer (optional)
- Basting Brush (optional)
- Meat Chopper (optional)

Directions:

1. Heat medium skillet on medium high-heat. Melt butter and add onions and celery. Cook until onions are soft.
2. Add sausage and break it up into small pieces (a meat chopper makes quick work of this). Stirring occasionally, cook until browned. Add garlic powder, optional herbs, black pepper, salt, and broth (and add any other optional stuffing extras) and then stir. Heat to a low boil.
3. Remove from heat. Add stuffing and mix lightly.
4. Spray oil or brush butter inside of 7" accessory bucket or baking dish.
5. Fill prepared 7" accessory bucket or baking dish with stuffing and spread into an even layer. Cover with foil.
6. For Oven Style Air Fryers: Place the stuffing dish on lowest rack of the air fryer. For Bucket Style Air Fryers: place the stuffing dish in the air fryer.
7. Air Fry at 350°F/175°C for 10 minutes, covered with foil. Then remove foil and brush with melted butter. Leave the stuffing uncovered in the air fryer.
8. Continue to Air Fry for another 2-5 minutes or until the top is crisp to your liking. Remove from air fryer and serve warm.

Air Fryer Frozen Bagel Pizza Bites
Servings: 4
Cooking Time: 9 Minutes

Ingredients:

- 9 (170 g) Frozen Bagel Bite Pizza Snacks
- OPTIONAL ADDITIONS
- grated parmesan
- red chili flakes
- EQUIPMENT
- Air Fryer

Directions:

1. Place the frozen bagel bite pizza snacks topping side up, in a single layer, in the air fryer basket/tray. Don't overlap the bagel bite pizzas or else they won't cook evenly. No oil spray is needed.
2. Air Fry at 360°F/182°C for 4 minutes. Check them for doneness.
3. Continue to Air Fry at 360°F/182°C for another 1-5 minutes or cooked to your preferred texture. Top with optional parmesan and/or red chili flakes if desired.
NOTES
Air Frying Tips and Notes:
No Oil Necessary. Cook Frozen - Do not thaw first.
Shake or turn if needed. Don't overcrowd the air fryer basket.
Recipe timing is based on a non-preheated air fryer. If cooking in multiple batches of pizza rolls back to back, the following batches may cook a little quicker.
Recipes were tested in 3.7 to 6 qt. air fryers. If using a larger air fryer, the pizza rolls might cook quicker so adjust cooking time.
Remember to set a timer to shake/flip/toss as directed in recipe.

Air Fryer Taquitos And Charred Salsa
Servings: 4-6

Ingredients:

- Deselect All
- Salsa:
- 1 pound Roma tomatoes
- 1 small onion, cut into 8 wedges
- 1 serrano chile
- 1 clove garlic
- 1 tablespoon extra-virgin olive oil
- Kosher salt

- Taquitos:
- 1 cup chopped rotisserie chicken
- 1 cup (about 4 ounces) shredded Colby Jack
- One 4-ounce jar diced pimientos, drained
- 1 teaspoon dried oregano
- 1/2 teaspoon ground cumin
- 1/2 teaspoon paprika
- 1/4 teaspoon chili powder
- Kosher salt
- One 12.6-ounce package small "street-size" corn tortillas (24 tortillas)
- 1 cup refried beans
- Butter-flavored nonstick cooking spray
- Sour cream, for serving
- Shredded romaine lettuce, for serving

Directions:

1. Special equipment: A 6-quart air fryer
2. For the salsa: Preheat a 6-quart air fryer to 350 degrees F (see Cook's Note).
3. Combine the tomatoes, onion, chile, garlic and oil in a large bowl and toss to coat. Transfer to the basket of the air fryer and cook until the skin of the tomatoes and the chile are wrinkled and the onion and garlic are charred, about 10 minutes. Cool slightly.
4. When cool enough to handle, peel the skins from the tomatoes and discard. Remove the stem, seeds and skin from the chile and discard. Place the tomatoes, chile, garlic, onion and 1/4 teaspoon salt in a blender. Pulse until smooth. Set aside until ready to serve.
5. For the taquitos: Combine the chicken, cheese, pimientos, oregano, cumin, paprika, chili powder and 1/4 teaspoon salt in a large bowl and toss.
6. Working in batches, quickly run 4 tortillas under running water. Shake off excess water and place in the air fryer basket. Fry until softened and pliable, 15 to 30 seconds. Fill them while they are still warm: Spread 2 teaspoons refried beans over a tortilla, reserving a bit of bean to dab on the seal. Spread 1 1/2 tablespoons of the chicken filling over the beans. Roll the tortilla over the filling and seal tightly with a little refried bean.

Repeat with the remaining tortillas, beans and chicken.
7. Spray all sides of the taquitos generously with cooking spray. Place in the air fryer basket (work in batches if needed) and fry until golden brown and crispy, about 8 minutes. Serve warm topped with some of the salsa and sour cream and shredded lettuce.
8. Cook's Note
9. Depending on the size of the air fryer, you may need to cook the taquitos in batches. Extra salsa can be refrigerated in an airtight container for up to 2 weeks. The taquitos can be prepared in advance: Air fry them until lightly golden brown, about 4 minutes. Allow to cool. Place in a resealable freezer bag and freeze for up to 1 month. To reheat, wrap in a moist paper towel and microwave for 1 minute to defrost the filling. Place in the basket of a 6-quart air fryer preheated to 350 degrees and cook until crispy and golden brown, about 6 minutes.

Carrot Chip Dog Treats
Servings: 50
Cooking Time: 4 Hr

Ingredients:
- 6 large carrots, washed
- ½ teaspoon dried parsley (optional)
- ½ teaspoon dried turmeric (optional)
- ½ teaspoon dried dill (optional)
- Items Needed
- Mandolin (optional)

Directions:
1. Slice the carrots into ¼-inch-thick rounds or strips using a sharp knife or mandolin.
2. Steam the carrots: Place a steamer rack in a large pot filled with 2 inches of water. Bring the water to a simmer, then add the carrots. Cover the pot and steam for 4 minutes, or until just tender but not falling apart. Remove the carrots when done and allow them to cool.
3. Combine the herbs in a small bowl, then sprinkle over the carrots.
4. Place the carrots evenly between the Food Dehydrator trays.

5. Set temperature to 135°F and time to 4 hours, then press Start/Stop.
6. Remove when done, cool to room temperature on the trays, then serve to your pet.

Air Fryer Sausage And Peppers
Servings: 4
Cooking Time: 10 Minutes

Ingredients:
- 1 onion sliced
- 1 bell pepper sliced
- 1 pound sausage of your choice
- 2 tablespoons olive oil

Directions:
1. Preheat your air fryer to 400°F.
2. Toss peppers and onions with the oil and season with salt and pepper to taste. Place in the air fryer basket.
3. Nestle the sausage between the vegetables and cook for 10 minutes, flipping the sausages halfway through the cooking time.

Reheat Pizza In Air Fryer
Cooking Time: 5 Minutes

Ingredients:
- 2-3 slices pizza (see description in notes)

Directions:
1. Set the Air Fryer to 325 degrees Fahrenheit and reheat the pizza according to thickness and size. 4-6 minutes for thick crust, 3-5 minutes for medium crust, and 2-4 minutes for thin crust.
2. Add additional increments of 1-2 minutes if needed.
NOTES
Click here to print out the infographic on how to reheat pizza in an Air Fryer.
Thick Crust: 325 degrees for 4-6 minutes, adding increments of 1-2 minutes if needed.
Medium Crust: 325 degrees for 3-5 minutes, adding increments of 1-2 minutes if needed.
Thin Crust: 325 degrees for 2-4 minutes, adding increments of 1-2 minutes if needed.

It's ok to open and check the food while cooking with an Air Fryer. Always make sure you are cooking and reheating the food evenly and not over cooking or over browning.

Jalapeno Poppers
Servings: 12
Cooking Time: 25 Minutes

Ingredients:
- 12 jalapenos
- 8 oz cream cheese, room temp
- 1 garlic clove, minced
- ¼ tsp salt
- ¼ tsp ground black pepper
- 3 Tbsp green onion, chopped
- 1 cup shredded mild cheddar cheese
- 8 oz bacon, cooked and chopped
- 1 Tbsp Parmesan cheese, optional

Directions:
1. Preheat the oven to 400°F. Halve the jalapenos lengthwise. Remove and discard the seeds and membranes from the jalapenos.
2. In a large bowl, combine the cream cheese, garlic, salt, pepper, green onion, shredded cheese, and cooked bacon for the filling.
3. Fill the jalapeno halves with the mixture. Placed stuffed jalapenos on a baking sheet and bake at 400°F for 18-20 minutes, or until the cheese melts golden in color. Sprinkle Parmesan cheese over the poppers and serve.

Basic Air Fryer Hot Dogs
Servings: 4
Cooking Time: 5 Minutes

Ingredients:
- 4 hot dog buns
- 4 hot dogs

Directions:
1. Preheat an air fryer to 400 degrees F (200 degrees C).
2. Place buns in a single layer in the air fryer basket; cook in the preheated air fryer until crisp, about 2 minutes. Remove buns to a plate.

3. Place hot dogs in a single layer in the air fryer basket; cook for 3 minutes. Serve hot dogs in toasted buns.

Air Fryer Oven Corn Dogs

Ingredients:
- 3/4 cup yellow corn meal
- 3/4 cup all-purpose flour (plus some extra on a plate for coating hot dogs)
- 1 1/2 tablespoons sweetener
- 1 1/2 teaspoons baking powder
- 1/4 teaspoon salt
- 1 egg
- 1 cup buttermilk
- 1 1/2 tablespoons melted butter
- 8-12 hot dogs
- 8-12 wooden skewers

Directions:
1. Spray cooking oil Combine dry ingredients into a large bowl and whisk. Add wet ingredients and mix thoroughly.
2. Transfer the batter to a tall drinking glass. Grease the mesh rack with cooking spa. Or use perforated parchment paper, if available.
3. Dry the hot dogs with a paper towel. Roll in flour, lightly coating. Stick the skewer into the hotdog then submerge in the batter.
4. Place the hot dogs onto the mesh rack and cook for 12 minutes at 400 degrees.
5. Cool before serving.

Air Fryer Toasted Perogies Recipe
Servings: 6
Cooking Time: 12 Minutes

Ingredients:
- 1 bag store bought frozen Perogies
- 2 cups Italian-style bread crumbs
- 1 egg
- 1 cup buttermilk
- Olive Oil Spray
- Parmesan cheese optional

Directions:

1. Whisk together egg and buttermilk. Dip Perogi in the egg/milk mixture and then cover with breadcrumbs. Repeat with all perogies.
2. Add perogies to the air fryer basket and spray with olive oil spray. Close the fryer basket and press power. Set the temperature to 400 degrees F and time to 12 minutes. Halfway through, pause and turn the perogies over. Add additional spray, if needed.
3. Garnish with additional Parmesan cheese and serve hot.

Peanut Sauce Soba With Crispy Tofu
Servings: 4

Ingredients:
- 2 12.3-oz. packages extra-firm tofu, drained
- 3 tbsp. canola oil
- 2 tsp. grated garlic, divided
- 2 1/2 tbsp. low-sodium soy sauce, divided
- 3 tbsp. natural smooth peanut butter
- 1 tbsp. agave or honey
- 1 tbsp. fresh lime juice
- 1/4 c. hot water
- 1/4 tsp. grated ginger
- 1 tsp. sriracha
- 1 tbsp. toasted sesame oil
- 2/3 c. cornstarch
- 8 oz. soba noodles, cooked per package Directions:
- 5 oz. baby spinach

Directions:
1. Pat tofu dry with paper towels and cut into 3/4-inch cubes.
2. In small bowl, whisk together canola oil, half of garlic, and 1 tablespoon soy sauce. Transfer one-third to small baking dish, coating bottom evenly. Add tofu and pour remaining marinade on top. Gently turn tofu to coat and let sit at room temp 45 minutes.
3. In medium bowl, combine peanut butter, agave, and lime juice with remaining 11/2 tablespoons soy sauce. Gradually whisk in hot water to emulsify. Whisk in ginger, sriracha, sesame oil, and remaining garlic. Set aside.

4. Heat air fryer to 400°F. Carefully dredge marinated tofu in cornstarch, coating evenly and shaking off excess. Add tofu to air fryer basket, spacing apart. Air-fry, shaking basket twice, until golden brown and crisp, 15 to 18 minutes.

5. Meanwhile, in large bowl, toss warm soba noodles with baby spinach and peanut sauce. Serve topped with crispy tofu.

Air Fryer Jalapeño Poppers

Servings: 6-8

Ingredients:

- 12 jalapeño peppers
- 2 c. shredded sharp cheddar cheese (about 5 oz.)
- 4 oz. cream cheese, softened
- 2 tbsp. mayonnaise
- 4 slices bacon, cooked and crumbled
- 1/4 c. diced pickled jalapeños, drained
- 1/4 c. finely chopped red onion
- 1/2 tsp. salt, divided
- 1/2 tsp. smoked paprika, divided
- 1/2 tsp. garlic powder, divided
- 1/2 c. panko breadcrumbs
- Ranch dressing, for serving

Directions:

1. Cut the jalapeño peppers in half lengthwise. Use a spoon to scrape out and discard the seeds and ribs from the peppers. Set the halved peppers aside.

2. Stir together the cheddar, cream cheese, mayonnaise, bacon, pickled jalapeños, onion and 1/4 teaspoon each salt, paprika, and garlic powder in a medium bowl. Stir together the panko breadcrumbs, and the remaining 1/4 teaspoon each paprika and garlic powder in a small bowl.

3. Fill each pepper half with the cheese mixture, and place on a foil-lined rimmed baking sheet. Sprinkle the tops of the peppers evenly with the breadcrumb mixture.

4. Transfer half of the stuffed peppers to an air fryer basket sprayed with nonstick cooking spray and space evenly. Spray tops of peppers with cooking spray. Cook at 380° for 5 to 7 minutes, until the tops are browned and cheese mixture is melty.

5. Place the cooked peppers okra on a rimmed baking sheet and keep warm in a 200° oven while air-frying the remaining stuffed peppers.

6. Serve jalapeño poppers with ranch dressing, if you like.

Notes

Love spicy food? Stir a pinch of cayenne pepper into the cheese mixture to crank up the heat.

Curried Parsnip Soup

Servings: 4
Cooking Time: 20 Minutes

Ingredients:

- 3 large parsnips peeled
- 1 large potato peeled.
- 2 cloves garlic crushed
- 1 large onion diced
- 1-2 tbsp medium curry powder (use hot or mild if preferred)
- 1 vegetable stock pot
- 1 bunch fresh coriander
- 1.5 litres boiling water
- low calorie cooking spray

Directions:

1. Keep half of one parsnip aside. Chop the rest of the parsnips into 1 inch pieces. Add to a saucepan with the diced potato, onion, garlic, curry powder and stock pot. Stir in the boiling water and simmer for 10 minutes.

2. Chop the half parsnip you put aside, into 0.5cm dice. Add to an air fryer with some low calorie cooking spray and cook for 10 minutes until crisp.

3. After 10 minutes, finely chop the leafy part of the fresh coriander and add half to the sauce pan. Simmer for a further 10 minutes.

4. Blitz the soup until thick and creamy - you may need to add some extra boiling water if it is too thick. Add the remaining coriander leaves and blitz for a further few seconds.

5. Serve immediately, topped with the parsnip croutons and a sprinkle of curry powder!

Air Fryer Hot Dogs

Servings: 2
Cooking Time: 10 Minutes

Ingredients:
- Nonstick cooking spray
- 4 hot dogs
- 4 hot dog buns (top cut is best)
- 4 slices cheddar cheese, optional
- For serving
- Mustard
- Ketchup
- Pickles

Directions:
1. Spray the basket of an air fryer with nonstick spray.
2. Air fry the hot dogs:
3. Add your 4 hot dogs to the air fryer basket, leaving some space between each hot dog.
4. Air fry at 350°F for 5 minutes. When the hot dogs are done, they should be glistening hot and slightly browned in spots.
5. Toast the buns in the air fryer:
6. Remove hot dogs from air fryer basket using tongs or a fork and place each hot dog in a bun.
7. Simple Tip!
8. I prefer top-cut buns for this recipe. The buns stand up easier for better toasting.
9. Place 2 assembled hot dogs in the air fryer and cook for 90 seconds to toast the bun. The finished toasted bun will have a light toast on it and be slightly crispy on the edges.
10. If you are adding cheese to your hot dogs—add a slice of cheese in the middle each bun and top with hot dog. Air fry for 90 seconds and cheese will be melted, and the buns toasted.
11. Repeat with remaining hot dogs.
12. To serve:
13. Serve hot dogs immediately topped with your favorite hot dog toppings including mustard, ketchup, and pickles.

Air Fryer Fig And Camembert Phyllo Parcel

Servings: 4
Cooking Time: 10 Minutes

Ingredients:
- 1 camembert round
- 2 TBSP fig jam
- 5 sheets phyllo pastry
- ½ cup melted butter
- Preserved figs and flaked almonds to serve

Directions:
1. Score the top of the camembert then top with fig jam.
2. Brush each sheet of phyllo pastry with butter, and lay the 3 pieces one on top of another.
3. Wrap the camembert in the pastry.
4. Brush the remaining 2 sheets of phyllo with butter and tear into strips.
5. Arrange in rosettes on top of the camembert.
6. Bake at 160ºC for 10 mins until golden.
7. Remove from the Vortex / Duo Crisp and serve with preserved figs and lightly drizzle with fig syrup.

Sicilian Pizza

Servings: 8
Cooking Time: 25 Minutes

Ingredients:
- For the Dough
- 4 cups all purpose flour
- 3 tsp kosher salt
- 1 tsp granulated sugar
- 0.75 oz Fleischmann's® RapidRise® Yeast packet
- 1 1/2 cup lukewarm water up to 1 3/4 cup
- 6 tbsp quality oil to coat the bowl plus more for the pan
- For the Assembly
- 1 lb mozzarella cheese sliced (up to 2 lbs)
- 3/4 cup pizza sauce up to 1 cup
- l lb crumbled cooked Italian sausage
- pepperoni slices
- cooked bacon in bits

- 1 green pepper chopped
- 1/2 medium onion chopped
- grated parmesan cheese
- dried Italian seasoning

Directions:
1. For the Pizza Dough
2. Add all-purpose flour, salt, sugar and yeast to a large bowl and stir to combine.
3. Next, add 2 tbsp of oil to the lukewarm water then add enough water to dry ingredients until it becomes elastic and soft but not too sticky. Remove from the bowl and knead with a little flour and form a ball.
4. Take another large bowl and coat with 1-2 tbsp of olive oil. Add the dough to the bowl, cover with plastic wrap, and let rise in a warm area for an hour.
5. After an hour, add remaining 3 tbsp of olive oil to a 11x17 inch pan. Remove the dough from the covered bowl and, using your finger tips, press and spread out the dough allowing some of the oil to get on the top of the dough in the dimples. Add plastic wrap over the pan and allow it to rest again in a warm area for another hour.
6. To Assemble Pizza
7. Preheat the oven to 500 degrees or as high as your oven will go and set your rack on the lowest bottom position.
8. Top your pizza dough with mozzarella cheese leaving a 1 inch border uncovered. Add as much cheese as you prefer.
9. Spoon pizza sauce over the cheese in diagonal rows or in various spots on top of the dough.
10. Sprinkle sausage, pepperoni, bacon, green pepper and onion on top of cheese and sauce.
11. Finally sprinkle with grated parmesan cheese making sure to sprinkle even on the 1 inch border.
12. Sprinkle with a tiny bit of Italian seasoning.
13. Bake for 20-25 minutes or until the dough is very crisp and browned and the cheese is totally melted and golden and slightly browned bubbly (don't' burn!).
Notes

To Store: After you've had your fill, allow the remaining slices to cool down until the cheese has slightly hardened. Next, stack the slices in a large resealable bag and store in the refrigerator. Alternatively, you can stack the slices in between sheets of wax or parchment paper and then, wrap the pizza pile in plastic wrap. Pizza will stay fresh for up to 4 days.

To Reheat: My first suggestion is to use an air fryer! Yes, an air fryer. It returns the dough to the perfect crisp exterior that you remember from the first dining experience. Secondly I suggest using a conventional oven for a perfectly crisp outside, warm, saucy inside and a gooey layer of cheese. Preheat the oven to 350 degrees, line a baking sheet with parchment paper and arrange the slices on top. Mist or drizzle a bit of water (to add moisture) and cover loosely with foil. Bake until hot and melt, about 15-20 minutes.

Vortex Hassel Back Butternut
Servings: 2-4
Cooking Time: 22 Minutes

Ingredients:
- 1 small butternut
- Garlic thinly sliced
- Salt & pepper
- Fresh sage (or rosemary)

Directions:
1. Peel the butternut, cut in half & remove the seeds.
2. Place a skewer on either side of the butternut and cut down towards the base the skewers will ensure you do not cut right through the butternut.
3. Makes cuts ½ apart and continue until you have cuts across the entire length of the butternut.
4. Drizzle with olive oil, season with salt and pepper.
5. Place pieces of thinly sliced garlic between the slices of butternut.
6. Put the butternut in the Vortex basket (or Duo Crisp).
7. Set the Vortex (or Duo Crisp) to bake at 180C for 20 mins.

VEGETABLE & & VEGETARIAN RECIPES

Baked Potato In Air Fryer

Servings: 2
Cooking Time: 40 Minutes

Ingredients:
- ½ teaspoon salt
- ½ teaspoon ground pepper
- 2 medium-large russet potatoes skin on and washed
- 1 tablespoon olive oil + more for drizzling
- Optional toppings: butter, fresh chives, fresh cracked pepper, Greek yogurt/sour cream

Directions:
1. Preheat the air fryer to 400°F and spray the air fryer basket with nonstick cooking spray or drizzle with 1-2 teaspoons of olive oil.
2. Add the salt, pepper, and garlic powder to a small bowl and mix until well combined. Set aside.
3. Drizzle 1 tablespoon of olive oil over the russet potatoes. Use your hands to rub the oil into the potatoes.
4. Sprinkle the salt, pepper, and garlic powder over the potatoes. Again, use your hands to rub the spices into the potato skin.
5. Place the potatoes into the air fryer basket and cook for 30 minutes.
6. Check the potatoes after 30 minutes. If the potatoes are fork-tender they are done. If the potatoes still have some resistance when you poke them with a fork, flip them over and cook them for another 5-8 minutes.
7. Remove the potatoes from the air fryer and enjoy them with your favorite potato toppings.
Notes
How long the potatoes are in the air fryer depends on the size of the potatoes and how kind of air fryer you have. A medium russet potato should take around 30 minutes, additional time may be needed if the potatoes are bigger.

If you want to add more flavor or spice to your potatoes, you can add more dried spices to the salt, pepper, and garlic powder.
If your potatoes smoke in the air fryer, this is normal!

Air Fryer Tomatoes

Servings: 4
Cooking Time: 8 Minutes

Ingredients:
- 4 medium Roma tomatoes
- 1 tablespoon olive oil
- 1 clove garlic minced
- 1 teaspoon rosemary freshly chopped
- 1 teaspoon thyme freshly chopped
- Salt and Pepper to taste

Directions:
1. Wash and pat dry each tomato with paper towels. Then slice in half with a sharp knife, lengthwise.
2. In a medium bowl, or laying flat on a baking sheet, toss tomatoes with olive oil, then season with garlic, rosemary, and thyme.
3. Brush the bottom of the Air Fryer basket with olive oil, spritz with cooking spray, or line with a piece of parchment paper. Place tomato slices in the air fryer basket in a single layer.
4. Air fry at 380 degrees Fahrenheit for 8-10 minutes. If you want crispier tomatoes, depending on size of tomatoes, add a few additional minutes of cook time.
NOTES
Seasonings and Flavors: Sprinkle some parmesan cheese, fresh herbs, blue cheese, garlic powder, or Italian seasoning!
Varieties of Tomatoes: You can use several kinds of tomatoes for this recipe. For example, you can use grape tomatoes, beefsteak tomatoes, Campari tomatoes, plum tomatoes, cherry tomatoes, or whatever type of tomato you like!
Flavorful Tomatoes: To get super flavorful tomatoes, make sure you thoroughly coat the tomatoes in seasonings so that the flavor can

meld with the tomato's juices. In addition, using seasonal tomatoes gives you an amazing flavor on top of added seasonings!

Air Fryer Baked Potato
Servings: 1
Cooking Time: 30 Minutes-1 Hour

Ingredients:
- 1 baking potato (see recipe tips and weigh before cooking), scrubbed and dried
- light rapeseed, vegetable or sunflower oil
- salt and freshly ground black pepper
- For the cheddar and jalapeño topping
- small handful grated cheddar
- 1 ripe tomato, diced
- few green jalapeño pepper slices from a jar
- For the smashed avocado topping
- 1 small, ripe avocado (or a few frozen avocado slices)
- ½ lime or lemon, juice only
- handful mixed seeds, dukkah, za'atar or chilli flakes
- For the curried beans topping
- 227g tin baked beans
- ½ tsp curry powder
- natural yoghurt and lime pickle (optional), to serve
- Recipe tips

Directions:
1. Rub the potato all over with a little oil. If you like, rub a little salt over the skin – this will help give a crispier finish.
2. Put the potato in the air fryer and turn to 200C (you don't want to preheat, to avoid burning the skin before the inside is cooked.) Air-fry for 20 minutes, then turn the potato over. A small potato will take another 20 minutes or so, a large one another 25–30 minutes.
3. Check the middle is soft by poking a table knife into the centre – it should slide in easily. If it's not quite done, continue to cook for a minute at a time.
4. For the cheddar and jalapeño topping, mix the cheese, tomato and jalapeño slices, split

the potato and spoon the cheese mixture on top.
5. For the smashed avocado topping, mash the avocado with the lime or lemon juice, salt and pepper. Split the potato, spoon in the avocado mixture and scatter with the seeds or your choice of seasoning.
6. For the curried beans topping, heat the beans with the curry powder until hot but not boiling. Split the potato and pile on the beans. Top with dollops of yoghurt and lime pickle, if using.
7. Recipe Tips
8. Small potatoes, around 225g/8oz each, will be ready in 40 minutes. Large potatoes, around 350g/12oz each, will take 45–50 minutes to get soft inside.
9. You can speed up the cooking by microwaving your jacket potatoes first. Microwave on high power for four minutes, turn the potato over, and microwave for another four minutes. (If you are cooking two potatoes, you may need to microwave them for an extra 2 minutes.) Then cook in the air-fryer for 10 minutes to crisp up.
10. Look for potatoes labelled as bakers, or a floury variety, such as King Edward, Maris Piper, Vivaldi or Estima.

Loaded Air Fryer Smashed Potatoes
Servings: 4
Cooking Time: 20 Minutes

Ingredients:
- 1 pound baby potatoes
- 2 slices uncooked bacon
- ½ cup cheddar cheese shredded
- 1 green onion sliced
- ¼ cup sour cream
- salt and pepper to taste

Directions:
1. Preheat the air fryer to 390°F.
2. Place the bacon in the air fryer basket and cook for 6-7 minutes or until crispy.
3. Remove from the basket and place on a paper towel don't discard the bacon grease. Crumble the bacon and set aside for later.

4. Toss the potatoes in a medium bowl with the seasonings and bacon grease.

5. Place the potatoes in the air fryer basket and cook for 10-13 minutes or until fork-tender.

6. Using the bottom side of a measuring cup or glass gently crush the potatoes and top with cheese.

7. Cook for 2 more minutes or until cheese is melted.

8. Garnish with sour cream, bacon bits, and green onions.

Notes

Don't overfill the air fryer basket with potatoes as they will take up more space once smashed. Cook in batches if needed. Heat all batches together before serving for 3 minutes.

Grilled Spring Vegetable Pizzas

Servings: 8
Cooking Time: 8 Minutes

Ingredients:

- ¼ cup all-purpose flour, for dusting
- 1 premade pizza dough, cut into 2 pieces
- 2 tablespoons olive oil, divided
- ⅔ cup fresh mozzarella, freshly shredded
- ½ cup English peas
- 10 asparagus stalks, trimmed and cut into ½-inch pieces
- Freshly ground black pepper, as needed
- ½ cup whole milk ricotta
- 1 tablespoon fresh basil leaves, chopped
- 1 lemon, zested and juiced
- ½ teaspoon kosher salt
- ¼ cup fresh microgreens

Directions:

1. Sprinkle a flat surface with flour, then gently stretch the dough into 2 (7-inch diameter) circles.

2. Drizzle ½ tablespoon of olive oil on each piece of dough, then divide the shredded mozzarella between them, followed by the peas, asparagus, and a sprinkling of pepper.

3. Place the cooking pot into the base of the Smart Indoor Grill, followed by the grill grate.

4. Select the Air Grill function on medium heat, adjust time to 8 minutes, then press Start/Pause to preheat.

5. Place one of the pizzas onto the preheated grill grate, then close the lid.

6. Combine the ricotta, remaining 1 tablespoon of olive oil, basil, lemon zest and juice, and kosher salt in a bowl and whisk until very light and fluffy. Set aside.

7. Remove the pizza when done and dot with the ricotta mixture and microgreens, then cut and serve. Repeat the cooking process with the remaining pizza.

Air Fryer Fried Green Tomatoes With Vidalia Onion Relish

Servings: 4
Cooking Time: 10 Minutes

Ingredients:

- Vidalia Onion Relish
- 2 Vidalia onions
- ½ cup mayonnaise
- ½ cup rice wine vinegar
- 2 tablespoons brown sugar
- 2 tablespoons fresh chives, chopped
- Fried Green Tomatoes
- 1 large firm green tomato
- salt
- 1 cup buttermilk
- ¼ cup all-purpose flour
- ¾ cup panko bread crumbs
- black pepper , to taste
- oil, for spraying

Directions:

1. Vidalia Onion Relish

2. For the relish, in a medium bowl, mix onions, mayonnaise, rice wine vinegar, brown sugar and chives. Cover with plastic wrap and marinade for at least 2 hours.

3. Fried Green Tomatoes

4. For the fried tomatoes, using a mandolin, cut tomato into ¼ inch thick slices. Lay tomato slices in a shallow pan and sprinkle with salt. Place tomato slices in a colander and allow time for salt to pull out water, approximately 30 minutes. Place buttermilk

in a shallow bowl. In a shallow dish, mix flour, bread crumbs, and pepper. Dip tomatoes in buttermilk, then dredge in flour mixture.

5. Line air fryer basket with parchment paper. Working in batches of 4, spray both sides of tomato slices with oil and place in air fryer basket. Set temperature to 400 degrees, and air fry for 5 minutes. Turn slices, spray with oil and air fry for 5 minutes more. Set aside tomato slices and keep warm. Repeat with remaining tomato slices. Serve hot with relish on the side.

Roasted Rosemary Potatoes
Servings: 4
Cooking Time: 12 Minutes

Ingredients:
- 1 pound fingerling potatoes, quartered
- 1 sprig fresh rosemary leaves, removed from stem and chopped
- 1 tablespoon olive oil
- 1 teaspoon garlic powder
- 1 teaspoon kosher salt
- ½ teaspoon black pepper

Directions:
1. Select the Preheat function on the Air Fryer, adjust the temperature to 400°F, then press Start/Pause.
2. Place all of the ingredients in a medium bowl and toss together until the potatoes are evenly coated.
3. Place the potatoes into the preheated air fryer basket.
4. Set the temperature to 400°F and time to 12 minutes, then press Start/Pause.
5. Shake the potatoes halfway through the cooking time.
6. Remove the potatoes when done and serve.

Buffalo Cauliflower Bites
Servings: 4
Cooking Time: 20 Minutes

Ingredients:
- 1 cauliflower

- 150 g flour
- 1 tsp paprika
- 1 tsp black pepper
- 1 tsp garlic powder
- 3 tbsp hot sauce
- 3 tbsp margarine

Directions:
1. Mix together in a large bowl (big enough to add all the cauliflower bits) Add the flour paprika, garlic and pepper then add around 6 tbsps, of water a couple at a time – until you have a thick batter, whisk till smooth
2. Preheat the air fryer to 200 degrees
3. Then add in the cauliflower pieces, and stir together till all the cauliflower is coated in the mixture
4. Add a few bits to the air fryer so they don't touch each other, best to cook in a few batches so they get an even cook
5. And cook for around 6/7 minutes – until you can shake the drawer and hear them crisp up! - give the drawer a shake around half way through
6. Make the buffalo coating, heat the hot sauce, toss the fried cauliflower pieces in the sauce .

Air Fryer Pickles
Servings: 8
Cooking Time: 5 Minutes

Ingredients:
- 4 large dill pickles
- 1/4 cup flour
- For the batter
- 1 large egg
- 1 tablespoon mustard
- 1 tablespoon mayonnaise
- 1/2 cup water
- 1/3 cup flour
- For the dry mix
- 1/2 cup breadcrumbs
- 1/2 cup panko breadcrumbs
- 1/2 teaspoon smoked paprika
- 1/4 teaspoon salt

Directions:
1. Preheat the air fryer to 200C/400F.

2. Slice the pickles in ½ inch slices and toss them in the flour.

3. In a small bowl, whisk together the egg, mustard, mayonnaise, and water. Slowly fold in the flour, until a smooth pancake-like batter remains. In a separate bowl, whisk together the dry mix.

4. Dip the pickles in the first batter, then the dry mix. Place the battered pickles on a plate lined with parchment paper.

5. Generously grease an air fryer basket. Place the pickles in a single layer and air fry for 4-5 minutes, or until golden brown.

6. Remove them from the air fryer and repeat the process until all the pickles are air fried.

Notes

TO STORE: Place leftovers in a shallow container and store them in the refrigerator for up to three days.

TO FREEZE: Place the cooled air fried pickles in a ziplock bag and store them in the freezer for up to two months.

TO REHEAT: These pickles are supposed to be crispy, so do not reheat them in the microwave. Instead, use a preheated oven or back in the air fryer.

Air Fryer Beignets

Servings: 20

Ingredients:

- Deselect All
- 2 cups all-purpose flour, plus more for working the dough (see Cook's Note)
- 6 tablespoons granulated sugar
- One 1/4-ounce packet instant yeast (2 1/4 teaspoons)
- 1/2 teaspoon kosher salt
- 1 large egg plus 1 yolk
- 1/2 cup lukewarm whole milk (about 110 degrees F)
- 3 tablespoons unsalted butter, melted, plus more for the bowl
- 1 teaspoon pure vanilla extract
- Nonstick cooking spray, for the beignets
- Confectioners' sugar, for dusting

Directions:

1. Special equipment: a 3.5-quart air fryer

2. Combine the flour, granulated sugar, yeast and salt in the bowl of a stand mixer fitted with the dough hook and mix to combine. Add the egg, egg yolk, milk, butter and vanilla and mix on low to combine. Increase the speed to medium high and knead until the dough forms a loose ball around the hook and is smooth and elastic, about 3 minutes.

3. Transfer the dough to a floured surface and lightly knead by hand just enough to bring it together into a smooth ball. Brush a medium bowl with melted butter and add the dough, turning to coat. Cover and let rise in a warm area until doubled in size, 1 hour to 1 hour 15 minutes.

4. Punch the dough down and roll out on a lightly floured surface to a slightly larger than 10-inch square. Trim the edges with a sharp knife or pizza cutter to make an even square. Cut the square in a 4 by 5 grid pattern to make 20 rectangles. Loosely cover the dough and let rise right on the countertop for about 15 minutes.

5. Preheat a 3.5-quart air fryer to 350 degrees F. Add half the beignets and spray them lightly with cooking spray. Cook until puffed and golden, about 6 minutes. Remove and repeat with the remaining beignets. Dust the beignets with confectioners' sugar and serve warm.

NOTES

When measuring flour, we spoon it into a dry measuring cup and level off excess. (Scooping directly from the bag compacts the flour, resulting in dry baked goods.)

Air Fryer Mexican Street Corn

Servings: 4
Cooking Time: 10 Minutes

Ingredients:

- 4 corn on the cob
- 1 teaspoon chili powder
- 2 Tablespoons cilantro fresh, chopped
- 1/2 teaspoon salt
- 1/2 teaspoon ground black pepper

- 1/2 cup Feta cheese
- 1 teaspoon lime juice freshly squeezed, optional

Directions:
1. Add the corn to the prepared air fryer basket.
2. Brush both sides of the corn with the melted butter.
3. Air Fry the corn at 400 degrees Fahrenheit for 10 minutes, flipping the corn halfway through the cook time.
4. Add the chili powder, salt, and pepper to the remaining butter. Mix until combined.
5. Brush the seasoned butter onto the cooked corn. Top the corn with the crumbled Feta cheese and then garnish with fresh cilantro and lime juice before serving.
NOTES
All air fryers are manufactured differently and cook differently. This recipe was made using a Cosori 5.8 qt air fryer. If you're using a different air fryer, you may need to add or take away a minute to ensure this recipe is fully cooked. I would recommend checking the recipe for doneness with 1-2 minutes remaining in cook time.
What cheese substitution can I use on Mexican Street Corn?
Most recipes call for Cotija cheese, but you can also use Feta cheese and parmesan cheese.
How long do I cook corn in the air fryer?
Corn is perfectly cooked and roasted when cooked at 400° Fahrenheit for 10 minutes in the air fryer.
Can you make a sauce for Mexican Street Corn?
Yes! While this recipe doesn't call for a sauce, some recipes do! You can use mayonnaise, sour cream, or even plain greek yogurt as your base and add the seasonings to it before brushing it on the cooked corn.

Air Fryer Buffalo Cauliflower Wings
Servings: 6
Cooking Time: 30 Minutes

Ingredients:
- For the Cauliflower
- 4 cups cauliflower florets ~1 medium head
- 1 cup blanched superfine almond meal
- 1 tablespoon garlic powder
- 1/2 teaspoon smoked paprika
- 1/2 teaspoon salt
- 1/2 teaspoon ground pepper
- 2 large eggs
- For the Buffalo Sauce
- 3 tablespoons melted butter
- 1/2 cup Franks Hot Sauce
- 2 tablespoons honey

Directions:
1. First, prepare cauliflower by cutting it into small, bite-sized pieces.
2. Next, place almond meal, garlic powder, paprika, salt, and pepper into a medium bowl and whisk to combine. Whisk 2 eggs in another medium bowl.
3. Prepare cauliflower wings by tossing cauliflower pieces in the egg wash to fully coat them. Then, place a couple of pieces of cauliflower into the almond meal bowl at a time. Use a spoon to carefully spoon the mixture on top of the cauliflower, coating it fully. Repeat until all cauliflower is coated in the mixture.
4. Preheat the air fryer to 370°F and spray the pan with nonstick cooking spray. Once preheated, place half of your cauliflower wings onto the bottom of the pan and spray the tops with nonstick cooking spray. It's okay if they are touching, but you'll have to cook these wings in 2 separate batches.
5. Air fry cauliflower wings at 370°F (or 375°F depending on the air fryer) for 12-15 minutes, tossing halfway through. You know your wings are done when they begin to brown and crisp up.
6. While your wings are air frying, prepare buffalo sauce. Melt 3 tablespoons of butter and then mix it with Frank's Hot Sauce and honey. Stir to combine.
7. Once your wings are done air frying, toss them in the buffalo sauce.
8. Serve immediately with your favorite dipping sauce.

Air Fryer Roasted Pumpkin

Ingredients:
- Cubed Pumpkin
- All Spice
- Sal and Pepper
- Cooking Oil
- Feta Cheese
- Spring onion

Directions:
1. In a bowl add the pumpkin, drizzle some all spice, salt and pepper to taste and drizlle some cooking oil. Select "roast" on your air fryer, set at 180C for 15 minutes, once preheat is done add your pumpkin. Once done, for colour and flavour, add spring onion and feta cheese.
2. Serve with a protein of your choice.

Mini Air Fryer Hasselback Potatoes
Servings: 4
Cooking Time: 10 Minutes

Ingredients:
- 1 pound small golden potatoes (about 1.5" long)
- olive oil spray

Directions:
1. Slice each potato ~10 times, making sure not to cut all the way through the potato. You want to have no larger than ¼" slices that go no more than ¾ of the way through the potato.
2. Add the potatoes cut side up to the air fryer (make sure not to overcrowd the air fryer basket) and spray them with olive oil spray. Season as desired (see notes for flavor suggestions).
3. Cook at 400°F for 10-12 minutes or until the potatoes are crisp and golden brown. Serve warm or store in an airtight container in the fridge for up to two days.
Notes
Serving Suggestions
Ranch: Sprinkle a pinch (about ¼ teaspoon) of dried ranch seasoning over each potato in Step 2.

Garlic Parmesan: Combine ½ cup grated parmesan and ¾ teaspoon garlic powder in a small bowl. Top each potato with 1 teaspoon of the mixture in Step 2.
Plain: Sprinkle a small pinch (about ⅛ teaspoon) of kosher salt over each potato in Step 2.
These potatoes will keep in the refrigerator for up to 4 days.

Air Fryer Frozen Vegetables
Servings: 4
Cooking Time: 10 Minutes

Ingredients:
- 1 pound mixed vegetables frozen
- 1 Tablespoon olive oil
- 1 teaspoon Italian seasoning
- 1/2 teaspoon ground black pepper
- 1/2 teaspoon sea salt

Directions:
1. Preheat the air fryer to 375 degrees Fahrenheit. If needed, prepare the basket with a non stick cooking spray such as olive oil.
2. Add the frozen vegetables to a small bowl and then add the olive oil, Italian seasoning, salt, and pepper. Mix well.
3. Add the seasoned frozen vegetables to the air fryer basket. It's ok to overlap the vegetables slightly, but try and keep as much room around them as possible to help with the cooking process. If you're using a small amount of vegetables, keep them in a single layer.
4. Cook the veggies at 375 degrees Fahrenheit for 5 minutes. Remove the basket and flip the vegetables. Then continue air frying for an additional 4-6 minutes of cooking time. Check the last two minutes to make sure they are done to your likeness and add additional time in one-minute increments if needed.
5. Carefully remove the vegetables from the basket of the air fryer and serve immediately.
NOTES
This recipe was made using a Cosori air fryer. If you're using a different air fryer model, you may need to adjust the cooking time slightly.

If you have a small basket, you may need to cook your vegetables in batches. For best results, try to keep the vegetables in a single layer.

Healthy vegetables are a great side dish for main course dishes such as air fryer steak, air fryer chicken, air fryer pork tenderloin, or even to serve with pasta.

You will want to adjust the cooking time down a few minutes for raw, fresh produce, and check on the vegetables after 5 minutes.

Air Fryer Potato Wedges
Servings: 4
Cooking Time: 30 Minutes

Ingredients:
- 3 small russet potatoes skin on
- 3 tablespoons olive oil
- 1 teaspoon garlic powder
- ½ teaspoon parsley
- ½ teaspoon seasoned salt
- pepper to taste

Directions:
1. Preheat air fryer to 400°F.
2. Scrub the skin of the potatoes and cut them in half lengthwise. Place them cut side down on a cutting board. Cut each half into four wedges (five wedges if they're really large).
3. Fill a large bowl with cold water and soak wedges for 30 minutes (optional, this removes starch from the potatoes). Drain very well, and dab potatoes dry with a kitchen towel or paper towel.
4. Toss the potato wedges with oil and seasonings.
5. Place in a single layer in the air fryer basket and cook 15 minutes. Shake the basket and cook an additional 10-12 minutes tossing every 5 minutes or so until crisp.
Notes
Be sure to dry the potatoes well before cooking so they crisp instead of steam.
Preheat the air fryer for best results.
Avoid crowding the basket so the wedges can cook evenly. If needed, cook potatoes in batches. Once all batches are cooked, add all

wedges to the air fryer for 2-3 minutes to heat through.
Leftover wedges can be reheated in the air fryer for 3-5 minutes.

Crispy Brussel Sprouts With An Asian Dressing
Servings: 4-6
Cooking Time: 13 Minutes

Ingredients:
- 800g Brussel Sprouts
- Sauce
- 3 Tbsp honey
- 1 Tbsp Smoked Chilli Flakes*
- 3 tbsp lime Juice
- 1Tsp zest
- 2 tsp sesame oil
- Salt to taste
- Oil, Salt and pepper as needed
- Chili flakes can be omitted

Directions:
1. Pressure cook phase:
2. Pour in 1 cup water into the inner pot. Add a good pinch of salt. Add the brussle sprouts. Set to Steam for 3 mins and once time is up do a Quick Pressure Release. When pin drops open lid and drain, then flush with cold water.
3. Air Fry phase
4. Toss the sprouts in a little cooking oil, then season them with a pinch of salt. Place the sprouts in the Instant Pot Vortex or Duo Crisp and air fry for 12-16 minutes or until golden brown.
5. While the spouts get crispy, make your dressing. Add the ingredients to a bowl and whisk to combine. Taste the dressing, add a pinch of salt to taste, then taste again. You can add more lime or honey depending on your preferences.
6. Once the sprouts are crisp, toss them in dressing and serve immediately.

Air Fried Crunchy Onion Rings

Servings: 6
Cooking Time: 20 Minutes

Ingredients:
- 1 cup all-purpose flour
- 1 teaspoon paprika
- 1 teaspoon salt, divided
- 1 cup buttermilk
- 2 eggs
- 2 cups panko breadcrumbs
- 2 large sweet onions, sliced 1/2-inch thick and separated into rings
- Oil Spray

Directions:
1. In a shallow bowl combine flour, paprika, and ½ teaspoon salt. In another bowl combine buttermilk and egg. In the third combine panko breadcrumbs and remaining ½ teaspoon salt.
2. Pat dry the onion rings with paper towels to remove excessive moisture. Dredge the onions in the flour mixture, drop them in the egg mixture and then dredge them in the panko mixture.
3. Arrange in a single layer on a dark-coated, non-stick baking sheet. Coat liberally with oil spray.
4. Air Fry at 400°F for 10 minutes, flip, cook 5 minutes more. Serve immediately with dipping sauce of your choice.

Air Fryer Broccoli

Servings: 8
Cooking Time: 8 Minutes

Ingredients:
- 2 heads broccoli chopped into bite sized pieces
- 2 tablespoons olive oil
- 1 tablespoon sugar
- 1/2 teaspoon salt
- 1/2 teaspoon pepper
- 1/4 teaspoon red pepper flakes optional

Directions:

1. Add the broccoli into a mixing bowl. Toss through the olive oil, then sugar, salt, pepper, and red pepper flakes.
2. Preheat the air fryer to 200C/400F for 5 minutes.
3. Add the broccoli and cook for 8 minutes, flipping halfway through.
Notes
TO STORE: Put the leftovers in the airtight container and store in the refrigerator for up to 5-7 days.
TO FREEZE: Place the cooked and cooled broccoli in a ziplock bag and store it in the freezer for up to 6 months.
TO REHEAT: Reheat in the oven, skillet or air fryer.

Crispy, Cheesy Cauliflower Balls

Ingredients:
- 300g cauliflower florets - steamed
- Handful Freshly chopped Spring Onion
- 2 cloves garlic - crushed
- 1 cup grated Mozzarella
- 60g Hard grated Cheese / Parmesan
- 1 Large Egg
- 1/2 cup breadcrumbs
- 1 T smoked Chilli flakes
- Salt & Pepper

Directions:
1. Steam the cauliflower - Once cooked place in a bowl and mash with a fork. You could use a food processor or mash until your desired consistency is reached. I prefer them to have a bit of integrity so I lightly mashed mine.
2. Add all the ingredients to the bowl and mix well. Mould the batter into balls - I suggest golf ball size. Using your Instant Pot Air Fryer - Preheat to 191C and bake for 20min - turning the balls halfway through. Serve with a dip or as a side and enjoy!

Baked Vegetable Crisps

Servings: 3-4
Cooking Time: 10-30 Minutes

Ingredients:

- 2 beetroot, scrubbed and very thinly sliced on a mandolin or with a vegetable peeler
- 2 carrots, scrubbed and very thinly sliced on a mandolin or with a vegetable peeler
- 1 large parsnip, scrubbed and very thinly sliced on a mandolin or with a vegetable peeler
- 1 tbsp light rapeseed, vegetable or sunflower oil
- ½ tsp dried oregano or herbes de Provence (optional)
- ¼ tsp garlic granules or powder (optional)
- salt and freshly ground black pepper

Directions:

1. Lay the vegetables on a tray and pat dry using kitchen paper or a clean tea towel. If you have time, leave them sandwiched in kitchen paper for 5–10 minutes to really dry out – this will give a crisper result.
2. Preheat the oven to 190C/170C Fan/Gas 5.
3. Put the vegetables in a big bowl, drizzle over the oil and some salt and pepper and mix with your hands, working the oil through thoroughly until all the vegetables are coated. Spread the vegetables evenly on two baking trays. Bake for 15 minutes, then turn over and bake for a further 8–12 minutes until dried out and golden brown.
4. Scatter with the herbs and spices, if using, and leave to cool and crisp up before serving.
NOTES
These are best eaten on the day you make them, but you can store them in an airtight container for up to 3 days. To serve, put them into a hot oven for about 3 minutes to crisp up. After this second baking they should stay crisp for the rest of their shelf life.
To air-fry, follow step 1, then mix the veg slices and peelings with the oil, salt and pepper. Air-fry in small batches at 180C for 5–7 minutes or until dry and browning. The parsnip and smaller beetroot crisps might be done first. Leave to crisp up on trays or plates while you cook the rest. When all the crisps are done, mix together the herbs and spices, scatter over and gently stir to coat.
To avoid food waste, you can make crisps from any kind of potato or root veg peelings. Season and oil as above, then cook for 12–15 minutes in a preheated oven at 190C/170C Fan/Gas 5, turning halfway, or 8–10 minutes in an air fryer at 180C.

Lamb Chops With Roast Potatoes And Chilli Mint Sauce

Servings: 3-4
Cooking Time: 25 Minutes

Ingredients:

- Potatoes
- 750g baby potatoes, halved
- 1 Tbsp olive oil
- 1 Tbsp chopped rosemary
- salt and pepper to taste
- Chops
- 6 lamb rib chops
- 1 Tbsp olive oil
- 1 Tbsp thyme leaves
- 1/2 Tbsp lemon juice
- 1 clove garlic, minced
- 1 tsp cumin seeds
- 1 tsp lemon zest
- salt and pepper to taste
- Sauce
- 50g fresh mint
- 5 rosemary sprigs
- 1/4 cup olive oil
- 2 Tbsp lemon juice
- 1/2 tsp chili flakes
- salt and pepper to taste
- To serve
- 250g tenderstem broccoli

Directions:

1. On the Vortex Plus ClearCook Dual, set drawer 1 to Grill* mode at 8 min and drawer 2 to Air Fry at 200C at 20 minutes; press Sync Finish so both drawers finish at the same time. Press Start and allow preheating to commence.
2. For the potatoes toss all the ingredients together to coat. When drawer 2 is ready, add

the potatoes and allow to cook, tossing halfway.

3. In the meantime, mix all the ingredients for the chops and coat them well. When drawer 1 is ready, add the chops and Grill for 8 minutes, turning halfway.

4. Blitz together all ingredients for the sauce to achieve a chunky consistency. When they are done, remove the chops from the drawer.

5. Reset this drawer to Air Fry at 180C for 5 minutes and add the broccoli. Cook the broccoli while the chops rest, tossing through the left-over lamb spices in the basket.

6. Serve the chops with crispy roast potatoes, broccoli, and a drizzle of chilli mint sauce. Enjoy!

7. *Grill mode automatically sets the Vortex to the highest temperature 205C for best results.

Air Fryer Cauliflower Buffalo Wings

Servings: 4-6
Cooking Time: 30 Minutes

Ingredients:
- 1 large head cauliflower, broken into 1-inch florets
- 2 eggs
- 1 cup plain breadcrumbs
- Non-stick cooking spray
- 1 cup Franks hot sauce
- 1/4 cup butter, melted
- 1/2 teaspoon kosher salt
- 1/2 teaspoon garlic powder
- 1/2 teaspoon black pepper
- Optional:
- Blue cheese sauce, for dipping
- Fresh carrots and celery, on the side

Directions:
1. Break apart the cauliflower
2. Cut the green stems back on the cauliflower head and then break or cut the head into about 1-inch florets. It's easiest to start near the base of the cauliflower and work your way toward the center.
3. Dip in egg wash and breadcrumbs

4. In a bowl large enough to hold the florets, whisk together 2 eggs and 1/4 cup of water. Add the florets to the egg mixture.

5. Use a slotted spoon to stir the florets making sure each is well coated. Remove the florets from the egg mixture and add them to the breadcrumbs. Toss them around until they are well coated.

6. Air fry the breaded cauliflower

7. Spray the air fryer basket with nonstick spray. Place the breaded florets in a single layer in the basket. Try not to crowd them. Set the air fryer to 350 F and fry the cauliflower for 7 minutes. Flip each floret and fry for another 7 minutes. Transfer to a platter.

8. Repeat this process until all the cauliflower have been fried.

9. Make the buffalo sauce

10. In a small bowl, combine the hot sauce, melted butter, salt, garlic powder and black pepper.

11. Coat the fried cauliflower

12. Dunk the florets of breaded and fried cauliflower one at time with a light coat of sauce. Return the pieces to the air fryer in a single layer and fry for another 4 minutes. Transfer to a platter.

13. Repeat the frying process with all your florets.

14. Serve

15. Serve the florets warm with blue cheese sauce, leftover buffalo sauce, and vegetables on the side.

Roasted Broccolini And Mushrooms With Salsa Macha

Servings: 4

Ingredients:
- 1 1/2 lb. oyster mushrooms, separated
- 2 1/2 tbsp. olive oil, divided
- Kosher salt and pepper
- 2 bunches Broccolini, trimmed and cut into large florets
- 1 c. fresh ricotta
- 1 tsp. lemon zest
- Milk, as needed

- 3 tbsp. salsa macha (we used La Comandanta)

Directions:
1. Heat oven to 425°F. On large rimmed baking sheet, toss mushrooms with 11/2 tablespoons oil and 1/4 teaspoon each salt and pepper and roast 8 minutes.
2. On second baking sheet, toss Broccolini with remaining tablespoon oil and 1/4 teaspoon each salt and pepper. Toss mushrooms, add Broccolini to oven, and roast both until golden brown and tender, 10 to 12 minutes more.
3. In bowl, mix ricotta and lemon zest, adding milk so mixture is smooth. Spread onto large plate or platter.
4. Arrange Broccolini and mushrooms on top of ricotta, then spoon salsa macha on top.
5. AIR FRYING:
6. Heat air fryer to 400°F. In large bowl, toss 10 ounces oyster mushrooms (separated) with 1 tablespoon olive oil and pinch each salt and pepper. Air-fry 5 minutes; shake basket and air-fry 3 minutes more. In same large bowl, toss 2 bunches Broccolini (trimmed and cut into large florets) with 1 tablespoon oil and 1/4 teaspoon each salt and pepper. Add to air-fryer (with the mushrooms) and air-fry until just tender, 5 minutes. Continue with steps 3-4.

Air-fryer Cauliflower Gnocchi With Marinara Dipping Sauce
Servings: 8

Ingredients:
- 2 (10 ounce) packages frozen cauliflower gnocchi, thawed, divided
- 3 tablespoons extra-virgin olive oil, divided
- ½ cup grated Parmesan cheese, divided
- 2 tablespoons chopped fresh flat-leaf parsley
- 1 cup reduced-sodium marinara sauce, warmed

Directions:

1. Preheat air fryer to 375 degrees F. Toss 1 package gnocchi, 1 1/2 tablespoons oil and 2 tablespoons Parmesan together in a large bowl.
2. Coat the basket of the air fryer with cooking spray. Transfer the gnocchi mixture to the basket; cook for 5 minutes, turning once halfway through. Transfer to a large bowl. Repeat the procedure with the remaining gnocchi and oil and 2 tablespoons Parmesan. Sprinkle the cooked gnocchi with parsley and the remaining 1/4 cup Parmesan. Serve with marinara.

Air Fryer Zucchini
Servings: 4

Ingredients:
- 2 medium zucchini, sliced into 1/4" rounds
- 2 large eggs
- 3/4 c. panko bread crumbs
- 1/3 c. cornmeal
- 1/3 c. freshly grated Parmesan
- 1 tsp. dried oregano
- 1/4 tsp. garlic powder
- Pinch of crushed red pepper flakes
- Kosher salt
- Freshly ground black pepper
- Marinara, for serving

Directions:
1. Place zucchini on a plate lined with paper towels and pat dry.
2. In a shallow bowl, beat eggs to blend. In another shallow bowl, combine panko, cornmeal, Parmesan, oregano, garlic powder, and red pepper flakes; season with salt and black pepper.
3. Working one at a time, dip zucchini rounds into egg, then into panko mixture, pressing to adhere.
4. Working in batches, in an air-fryer basket, arrange zucchini in an single layer. Cook at 400°, flipping halfway through, until crispy on both sides, about 18 minutes. Serve warm with marinara.

Air Fryer Brussel Sprouts

Servings: 4
Cooking Time: 7 Minutes

Ingredients:

- 1 pound brussels sprouts halved, or quartered if extra large
- 1 tablespoon olive oil
- salt and pepper to taste

Directions:

1. Toss brussels sprouts with olive oil, salt, and pepper.
2. Cook in the Air Fryer at 375°F for 4 minutes.
3. Shake and cook for an additional 3 minutes, or just until tender.

Notes

Select Brussels sprouts that are similar in size. If you have some smaller and some larger, cut the larger ones in half.

Add any kind of seasonings you like. We love cajun seasoning and garlic powder.

A sprinkle of parmesan or a drizzle of balsamic glaze is great on these sprouts after they come out of the air fryer.

Air Fryer Asparagus

Servings: 4
Cooking Time: 8 Minutes

Ingredients:

- 1 pound asparagus
- 1 tablespoon olive oil
- 1/4 teaspoon kosher salt
- 1/4 teaspoon black pepper
- 1/4 teaspoon garlic powder

Directions:

1. Rinse the asparagus well. Trim the stems of the asparagus, cutting about 1-2 inches off the bottoms of each stem.
2. Brush with olive oil, covering the asparagus, then sprinkle salt and pepper, or desired seasonings on the asparagus.
3. Place asparagus in the air fryer basket.
4. Air fry asparagus at 400 degrees Fahrenheit for 8-10 minutes of cooking time, depending on desired crispness. Toss asparagus halfway during air frying.

NOTES

I trim the ends off of the asparagus before cooking them, so they are crisper and the same size for cooking. Most importantly, those ends are tough to chew, so it makes the asparagus easier to eat.

This simple vegetable side dish is so versatile and can be made with just simple seasonings, like salt and pepper, or fresh garlic. However, it's also delicious with a squeeze of lemon juice too!

Air Fryer Cauliflower

Servings: 4
Cooking Time: 14 Minutes

Ingredients:

- 1 head cauliflower cut into florets
- 2 tablespoons olive oil
- ½ teaspoon garlic powder
- salt & black pepper to taste
- ⅓ cup parmesan cheese finely shredded

Directions:

1. Cut cauliflower into florets. Wash and drain very well.
2. Combine olive oil, garlic powder, salt, and pepper in a small bowl. Toss with cauliflower.
3. Preheat air fryer to 390°F.
4. Place cauliflower in the air fryer basket and cook 12 minutes.
5. Sprinkle with parmesan and cook an additional 2-3 minutes or until florets reach desired doneness.

Notes

If the cauliflower is wet (after washing) it will steam instead of roast so be sure to drain very well. If possible, I try to wash the cauliflower the day before roasting.

For crispier cauliflower, cook in small batches in a single layer. Place all cauliflower in the air fryer together for 2 minutes before serving to heat.

To reheat, air fry 3-4 minutes or until heated through.

Printed in Great Britain
by Amazon

26064317R00064